THE NEXT FEW YEARS WILL CHANGE YOUR LIFE

THE NEXT
FEW YEARS
WILL
CHANGE
YOUR LIFE

TRAVIS HANSEN

WITH DICK HARMON

FOREWORD BY DAVE ROSE

DESERET
BOOK

SALT LAKE CITY, UTAH

Library of Congress Cataloging-in-Publication Data

Hansen, Travis, 1978– author.
  The next few years will change your life : create a plan, set goals, and find the hero within / by Travis Hansen with Dick Harmon ; foreword by Dave Rose.
      pages cm
  Includes bibliographical references.
  ISBN 978-1-60907-049-6 (paperbound)
1. Goal (Psychology) 2. Self-management (Psychology) 3. Success. I. Harmon, Dick, 1952– author. II. Title.
  BF505.G6H365 2012
  650.1—dc23   2012023817

Printed in the United States of America
Publishers Printing, Salt Lake City, UT

10 9 8 7 6 5 4 3 2 1

To my beautiful wife, LaRee,
and our three wonderful children:
Ryder, Mason, and Halle

Contents

Contents

Foreword

The things I remember most about Travis Hansen the basketball player are the same things that stand out today about Travis Hansen the world traveler, retired professional athlete, father, and husband. He is driven, he hates to lose, and he finds ways to motivate himself.

I first met Travis Hansen in 1996 when I was coaching at Dixie College and hoping to recruit him. I remember how determined Travis was and how motivated he was to get better every day. He was one of those guys who always talked about getting better. Of course, a lot of guys talk about it but then just go about their business and don't do anything to make it happen. Travis actually did what he said he would do.

When I began coaching at BYU, I helped recruit Travis. In 2000, almost immediately after coming to BYU to play, he injured his foot and had to wear a large, awkward boot.

In addition to the boot on his foot, he wore his feelings on his sleeve—and he was frustrated. Frustrated but happy.

Travis is extremely competitive. Most players are motivated because they love to win. Travis is motivated because he hates to lose, and he communicated that to his teammates throughout most of the games. I can relate to that because that's how I'm wired.

I'll never forget when Travis tore his Achilles tendon some seven years later while playing basketball in Russia. He e-mailed me with the news that he was flying home to Utah to have surgery. The day he got out of the hospital, I went to see him. During the two-hour visit, the conversation we had was typical of Travis. He was groggy, but he probably said five times during our visit, "I am going to come back from this, I will be back. They don't think I can come back and play, but I'm going to prove them wrong. I will be back."

He asked me if I knew other players who'd torn their Achilles and how long it had taken them to return—had it been nine months or a year? He vowed he would come back in six months and play again. He was very determined, and he did come back in six months and played the next year.

Travis is a very special individual. He may be known for his extraordinary drive as a basketball player, but that is only a small part of who he is.

While playing, he managed to build a charitable organization and accomplish an amazing amount of good. He has accomplished amazing things. He has an unusual work ethic and exceptional people skills. He has a delightful sense of humor and is very bright and creative.

I'm confident that reading what he has to say will be much like watching him play—entertaining, valuable, and perhaps even life changing.

DAVE ROSE

Preface

Travis Hansen is a positive-minded, fun-loving, highly competitive athlete who has played basketball with the best players on the planet. He's also a motivated, faithful, and fearless defender of the gospel of Jesus Christ, who has backed up his beliefs with action.

I first met Travis when he was just twelve years old on a trip down the Colorado River when his father, Scott, and I joined a few other dads in taking our sons on a three-day outing from Moab to Lake Powell on rubber rafts.

This book is not a biography of Travis, although I believe such a project would be more than worthwhile. This is a book that seeks to teach life lessons to young people about growing up, overcoming mistakes, setting goals, finding out who you are, avoiding addictions, and building faith in the Savior.

Travis is a gifted athlete who is blessed with the ability to soar on the basketball court. He has a vertical jump of forty inches, and at six feet six is 215 pounds of energy. A star at Mountain View High in Orem, Utah, Travis became a two-time All-Mountain West Conference player and was named Defensive Player of the Year in the league after he served an LDS mission to the Santiago Chile West Mission.

Travis helped BYU register a 44–1 home court record during his three years there, something that had never been done at the school. He was known as a lock-down defender on defense, a three-point threat as a shooter, and was good enough to play four positions on the court (point guard, shooting guard, and small and power forward). He could also post up as a center if needed.

The Atlanta Hawks made Travis a second-round pick in the 2003 NBA draft, a year that produced superstars LeBron James, Carmelo Anthony, Chris Bosh, and Dwayne Wade.

Travis left the NBA before his contract ended for an opportunity to play in Europe. He began his career overseas with Tau Cerámica in Spain before signing with Dynamo Moscow in Russia. He then played for Real Madrid in Spain before finishing with Khimki in Moscow, where he retired from basketball in September 2011.

Travis is one of the most faithful, engaging, uplifting people I have covered in thirty-seven years as a sports writer. His wife, LaRee, is an inspirational wonder. The good this couple has accomplished in such a short time in their lives is remarkable and motivating. Their devotion to their faith is infectious.

While in Russia, the Hansens founded the Little Heroes Foundation, which began work to refurbish and outfit a hospital for orphans. With the help of many kind and generous sponsors, the foundation has been instrumental in establishing schools, hospitals, and health clinics from Africa to Nepal and parts of South America. The people impacted by this work number in the tens of thousands.

Travis and LaRee currently live in Orem, Utah, with their three children. Travis is chairman of the Little Heroes Foundation.

It has been an honor and blessing to work with Travis and LaRee on this book, and I hope the messages conveyed are delivered in the spirit in which they have been told.

DICK HARMON

The Travis Hansen Timeline

1993–1996	Played for Mountain View High School in Orem, Utah
1996–1997	Played for Utah Valley State College in Orem, Utah
1997–1999	Served LDS mission in Santiago, Chile
2000–2003	Played for Brigham Young University
July 14, 2000	Married LaRee Merrell
January 23, 2003	Son Ryder was born
2003–2004	Played for NBA team Atlanta Hawks
2005–2006	Played for Tau Cerámica in Victoria, Spain
2006–2009	Played for Dynamo Moscow in Russia

February 2007	Tore Achilles tendon, requiring surgery
May 2007	Started Little Heroes Foundation
August 1, 2007	Son Mason was born
September 2007	Oversaw renovations at orphan hospital in Lyubertsy, Russia
2009–2010	Played for Real Madrid in Spain
May 2010	Injured back, requiring surgery
May 20, 2010	Adopted daughter Halle
2010–2011	Played for Khimki in Moscow, Russia
September 2011	Retired from basketball

Introduction

In the early summer of 2011, I flew across the Atlantic Ocean one last time as a professional basketball player. As my precious little girl, Halle, lay asleep across my lap, I thought of the last thirty-three years of my life: the failures, successes, experiences, relationships, and special moments. I looked at my handsome boys, my beautiful wife, and my sweet daughter, and I was thankful to have a healthy family. I was then overcome by the thought and uncertainty of my children's future. What would their lives be like? What challenges and trials would they face? Would they make good choices, have good friends, help others, be hardworking, and fully understand and love the gospel of Jesus Christ?

President Gordon B. Hinckley said: "In my quiet moments, I think of the future with all of its wonderful possibilities and with all of its terrible temptations. I wonder what will happen to you in the next 10 years. Where will you be? What will you be doing? That will depend on the choices you make, some of which may seem unimportant at the time but which will have tremendous consequences.

"Someone has said, 'It may make a difference to all eternity whether we do right or wrong today.'[1]

"You have the potential to become anything to which you set your mind."[2]

I'm writing this book because I believe there are experiences to share that may help young people who are making decisions about who they are and where they want to go in life. I want my children to make good choices, learn to set goals, and find their own talents to share with the world. The gospel is the center of my life, and I hope it will become the center of theirs—and yours. I want my children and the young people of the Church to understand how the gospel is not limiting; rather, it is capable of freeing you and leading you to true peace and happiness.

I have been blessed with the experience of traveling around the world and would love to share what my wife, LaRee, and our life experiences have taught me. I have met many wonderful people who have shared experiences that have changed my life. If, by writing this book, I can help one person to be stronger, make good choices, feel closer to Heavenly Father, and serve a mission, then I have accomplished my goal.

I have tried to improve my life every day. I've made mistakes and poor choices, but I've always woken up and had the desire to be better. I decided long ago I would never give up, never stop dreaming, believing, or working hard, and I would always try my best. I hope this book inspires you to do the same.

CHAPTER 1

The Backboard

For six hours one summer day I waited my turn in an inner city Los Angeles emergency room while medics brought in car accident and gunshot victims and pushed them ahead of me in line. My shoulder was bleeding, and I had shards of glass in my skin and hair.

Yeah, I was hurt. But I'd just been part of a life-changing event and had sacrificed some blood in the process.

It was July 1999 and I'd been off my two-year mission to Chile for all of about five days. I may not have been totally ready to play basketball, but I couldn't pass up the opportunity to at least get out and try. I was out of shape and about twenty pounds over my playing weight. My dad had bought me a ticket to fly to California and rented a car to take us to the gym.

The occasion was a basketball tournament at Santa Dominguez Community College where a lot of junior college and high school players had gathered to play against each other. The bleachers were filled with college recruiters from all over the country. They'd swooped down to inspect prospects, take a few notes, shake some hands, and wear their school colors like billboards. Stanford coach Mike Montgomery was there, as were BYU coach Steve Cleveland and his chief assistant Dave Rose, along with other Pac-10, Mountain West, and other conference coaches.

Utah Valley State College head coach Jeff Reinert had a bunch of his players in the tournament, and I'd been invited to join them and take on a team comprised primarily of local black athletes from Compton and the surrounding area.

Five minutes into the game, I'd hit a couple of three-point shots. I felt pretty good and was, frankly, surprised that my shot seemed to be coming back. But as defenders are prone to do, they began to close in on me and guard me more heavily once I hit those shots.

On another possession, coming down the court, the guy defending me came up and began to crowd my dribble. He wasn't going to give me any space to let another three-pointer fly. I decided to do something about it. I wasn't going to try and get off a jump shot. I was going to challenge him with my dribble on the left side of the key, and I made my move. A second later, I saw a path open up to the rim and I kept going as three defenders tried to cut me off and prevent me from getting an easy layup.

I charged to the basket, but the others had reacted too late.

Once I got inside the key, I reacted naturally. In high school, when I was in this kind of position, the decision of what to do was easy. I was going to dunk the ball. I was going to sail up as high as I could and slam the ball home.

A basketball rim is ten feet off the floor, which is 120 inches. If you are six feet six inches tall, the orange piece of steel is forty-two inches above your head. Add the length of your arms, and it comes a couple feet closer. To dunk the ball, you have to get your hands and the ball over the rim, so you must be able to jump high enough to be above the rim. If you can jump and get your feet forty inches off the floor, it really helps to complete the act of a dunk.

I jumped, got the ball high over the rim, and slammed it.

If you get up that high and there are sweaty defenders surrounding you, trying everything possible to stop you, the instinct is to hang on to the rim and make sure nobody takes your legs out from under you, crashing you to the floor where you could break a leg, your back, or your head.

Instinctively, without forethought or any plan at all, that is exactly what I did.

As I hung on the rim after the dunk, the two-hundred-pound tempered-glass backboard exploded. Fearing the steel rim would hit me in the head after I landed on the floor, I held on to the rim and my momentum brought it around, away from my head, and buried it into my shoulder, gashing the skin. I closed my eyes to protect them from the glass that flew around the gym like diamonds dumped on the court.

Everyone in the gym was stunned. So was I as trainers

and doctors came to my aid. They told me to keep my eyes closed as they brushed the glass from my eyes and face and took me in a back room for treatment. It goes without saying that nobody played any more basketball on that court for a few hours as organizers tried to find a replacement backboard and rim, and I was shuffled off to a nearby hospital.

As I left the gym, I kept hearing fans in the stands calling me "White Chocolate Thunder." They treated me like some kind of superstar.

"He's a beast," said one.

"He broke it, he broke the backboard!" said another.

"Hey, White Chocolate, way to go, man!" said a third guy.

It was crazy. After waiting my turn in the emergency room, they finally got me to a table where a doctor worked to get all the glass out of my wound. They flushed ten gallons of water on that wound trying to get out the tiny pieces. When I got back to the hotel to take a shower, there was still glass in my hair.

That single moment in time in the summer of 1999 kicked off an immediate recruiting battle for my services. Word spread quickly. The recruiters who were there couldn't get the image of the dunk and the exploding backboard out of their minds.

 Scan this QR code (or visit http://youtu.be/B2OWAx QcN2M) to hear Travis tell the story of how he broke the backboard.

I'd come off my mission with a dream to play Division I basketball. I didn't want to play another year of junior college. That day—those five minutes at that junior college, that rim, that backboard—was all it took. Within days, I had offers from Washington, UNLV, Utah, BYU, and a lot of other schools, and I didn't even have to play another game. I ended up signing to play for BYU.

There are a lot of defining moments in a person's life. For me, this was one of them. I took advantage of that day and it taught me a lesson: Any time opportunities present themselves, you can't waste them. You have to live life with no fear and no regrets. I didn't think twice about trying to dunk the ball that day; it came naturally because I was taught to believe in myself and doubt not (see Mormon 9:27).

The split-second decisions in the sequence of events that day were the product of thousands of hours of practice and reaction to situations on the basketball court. We do the exact same thing off the court in real life. Successful winners are made, not born.

What that shattered backboard did for me was part of a long line of events that have shaped my life. Any successes I've had have come through a lot of prayer, hard work, sacrifice, making mistakes, and learning from my errors and weaknesses.

To make it on and off the court means we must *believe* that it can be done. I look at the champions I've known. They have big dreams because big dreams are the only kind that produce the motivation, determination, and drive to succeed. It takes courage to follow dreams, regardless of how others judge you or your chances.

There is great wisdom in losing yourself in good things, in helping others, and in forgetting your own problems. There is a special power bottled up inside everyone. There is a piece of God that lies within all of us if we will just seek it, find it, and set it free. There are many examples of how to find that special power inside, and how to see that light in others you meet every day.

My greatest hero is Jesus Christ. The things He did, the miracles He performed, the life He led, the example He gave, the way He treated others—especially those who hated and mocked Him—lift me up. The teachings He left us are inspiring and uplifting and the perfect road map to happiness in this world and the world to come. "For God so loved the world, that he gave his only begotten Son, that whosoever believeth in him should not perish, but have everlasting life" (John 3:16).

Finding the hero within you means finding your true identity and discovering what abilities and talents you have. It's about finding what you are good at, what tools you have, and how best to use them. Finding the hero within you means finding your own true peace and happiness and helping others find theirs.

Whatever you do, don't be afraid to dream big. "If thou canst believe, all things are possible to him that believeth" (Mark 9:23).

CHAPTER 2

Music of the Bouncing Ball

In reality, the sound of a bouncing ball is a dull, lifeless kind of sound. But it is an echo—a cadence—that will stay with me forever. As a little kid growing up in Orem, Utah, that sound was music, a symphony! It inspired me, lifted my spirits, and energized my whole body, mind, and soul as it opened the door to a dream.

Like the kids at play who donned the role of a soldier in combat, or a cowboy on the frontier, or a fireman in a raging inferno, I'd step into a fantasy when I picked up a ball. Dribbling a basketball put me in a real dream state—a make-believe world where I was the hero who people in a packed arena expected to make the game-winning shot. Every day I'd go out on the driveway and place myself in this trance hundreds of times. I envisioned the screaming crowd standing on their feet, I'd see myself dribbling the ball against one of the NBA's superstars, making a move, getting open, pulling up, and shooting the big shot. Sometimes it would be a long, arcing three-pointer; sometimes it would be an inbound pass to me with seconds left on the game clock. Other times, I'd put the rim down so I could reach it, and I'd be big Shaquille O'Neal, getting a lob at the rim, turning, and jamming the ball home.

I created my own crowd in my mind. I also became my own sportscaster doing the play-by-play. I'd create a scoreboard clock, a score, and a situation to overcome or beat, and I'd work on that over and over again. In my dreams those days, with the sound of the ball echoing off the walls of the house, I imagined myself delivering the big play thousands of times. I did this every day of every year of my young life.

I don't know if every little boy does this. As an adult I look around my neighborhood and see kids following this routine. At times, my son Ryder is so enveloped in something when at play that I have to get right up in his face to break him out of the trance. I think this kind of make-believe play resonates with children. It did for me.

I grew up in a family where this was acceptable behavior and was encouraged. My family was very sports-oriented, and sports encompassed much of our spare time. My siblings had baseball, soccer, and basketball games and practices throughout the week, as well as on Saturdays.

My mother, the former Laurie Mitchell, was a high school track athlete from Richland High in Washington. She met my dad, a basketball player at Ricks College, when they both attended school in Rexburg, Idaho. They dated, my dad went on a two-year mission, and they married when he returned.

I have my mother's looks and definitely inherited many of her genes. My dad is six feet five, husky and strong, and built like a rock. My mother was sleek, skinny, and very fast. My facial features and personality are a good combination of both.

I had a great childhood growing up in Orem. I'd ride my bike to Trafalga Fun Center and play games or go to the park to play tennis, but my endless desire was to play professional basketball. Our driveway even had lines of a basketball court painted on it.

My dad, Scott Hansen, grew up on a farm in Idaho, and he is the hardest working man I know. He worked for an insulation company while going to school. When he finished his degree he started his own company in Price, Utah, called Hansen Insulation. He was a great father, always there for his children. He was supportive and very charitable and giving to others. He was a driven person. Every day he'd get up early and start knocking off items on his list. It was important for him to get things done, push things forward, show results at the end of the day. I remember how he'd get me and my brothers out of bed Saturday mornings to clean the garage. We'd have to do every corner and get it done right. If it wasn't done as well as he thought it should be, he'd make us come back time and time again until it was done correctly. Sometimes we'd protest and go to our mother and

The Hansen family.

complain. She was always the perfect mediator, telling us to stop complaining and go back to work when we needed but also knowing when to tell my dad we had worked enough for the day.

My dad had my brother Tyler and me paint the fence one summer and he had us out there making perfect up-and-down strokes with the brush. "Anything worth doing is worth doing well," he'd say.

Tyler loved baseball, lifting weights, and fly-fishing. He was a hard worker and a great older brother. Landon, who was next after me, was my clone. He acted like me, tried to be funny like me, and hung out with me and my friends, who would torture him. He was into many sports, especially golf.

After Landon came my two sisters, identical twins,

Heather and Hollie. They are the princesses of the family, and my parents treated them as such. Hollie was a tomboy who wore cowboy boots and had an attitude. Heather was a princess in every sense of the word and loved to do everything opposite of Hollie. I remember one time we were on a family vacation in Rexburg, Idaho, staying in a motel, and my mom yelled out to the girls, "Do you like the pool?"

Hollie answered, "I don't like this pool. This is not a cool pool."

Heather then answered, "I love this pool, Mom! This is the best pool!"

The twins ended up playing on state championship basketball teams at Mountain View High School and earned McDonald's All-American honors and scholarships to play basketball at BYU.

My father loved my mother with all his heart, and she loved my father the same. They created a home where the gospel was at the center of our lives and they always set an example for their children to live a good, honest life and love God. Our home was a popular hangout for our friends. Everyone loved to come to our house to eat, play games, and just visit. I guess my mother believed it was a good thing, not an imposition. After all, if all of us and our friends were hanging around our house, we wouldn't get in trouble.

My mom, with her great cooking and open invitation to all my friends; my dad, with his wisdom and work ethic; my brothers and sisters, with their enthusiasm and drive: these people made up the heart of our home—a safe haven, a place I return to often in my memories. And then there's the driveway, with its painted lines, its fence, and the sound of the bouncing ball. The hours I spent dribbling and dreaming are memories that will never die in my mind. Counting down the shot clock, five . . . four . . . three . . . two . . . one . . . , then the buzzer; me, trying to beat the buzzer, a shot that saved the day—it was my world, an existence I created so I could step into it and become what I hoped I would always be.

CHAPTER 3

Portsmouth

If you dare to dream, believe, and work hard, you can make nearly anything become a reality. At the foundation of that success is *commitment*. Hours and hours and hours of it. How do I know this? At first I didn't really *know* it. I only believed it. But because I believed it, I was able to do the work. And then, one day, in Portsmouth, Virginia, I had a glimpse of that success and knew the commitment would pay off.

I can remember only a handful of times I didn't wake up at 6 A.M. to go to the church and play basketball as a kid. My friend Ty Shippen and I loved to work at our game; we didn't shy away from it at all. We spent hours a day working out, pounding the pavement in my driveway or the hardwood in the gym. We'd rebound for each other while the other shot.

I was determined to do my best to reach my potential. I

Playing for BYU.

felt humbled and extremely blessed that I had a gift to play, the desire to practice, and an opportunity to succeed.

When I finished my career at BYU, I received an invitation to play in the Portsmouth Invitational in Virginia. Since 1953, the organizers of this springtime tournament have lined up sixty-four of the best college senior basketball players across the country to play in front of scouts, coaches, and general managers from every NBA team, as well as scouts from international leagues.

In fact, Portsmouth has been a showcase for five of the fifty greatest players in NBA history: Rick Barry, Earl "The Pearl" Monroe, Dave Cowens, John Stockton, and Scottie Pippen. Players are divided up and put on four teams; and as they play one another, scouts fill out notebooks and reports that will help them make decisions come draft time.

I remember getting on a plane for Portsmouth in Salt Lake City, feeling both nervous and excited as I claimed my seat next to Weber State star Jermaine Boyette.

"It's our time now. This is it," said Boyette. "No fear, give it all you have. This is our new life."

When we got to the gym, I felt ready to do just as Boyette had suggested—give it all. One of the first things organizers did was put us through drills. We ran v-cuts off the pick and catch-and-shoots. I seemed to be doing the drills with ease. As I looked around at some of the others, I was fairly surprised. A few looked confused; they stumbled a little and lost their timing. *Maybe a few are out of practice in the off-season*, I thought. My confidence began to grow. Many of those guys were from the ACC, Big Ten, SEC, Big 12, and Pac-10. A thought flashed through my mind: *I might actually be able to compete and play this game.*

When we began playing, I was on the bench. But I finally got the nod to go on the floor and play—and I played amazingly. I got a baseline drive and dunk, made a couple of three-pointers, and scored about fifteen points in ten minutes. I started in the next game, which we won. I developed a rapport with the two point guards on my team, which is always a good thing to do if you are a shooter. They fed me the ball perfectly many times over the course of the game. Chad Ford of ESPN came up to me after and said he was doing an NBA draft analysis on the best shooting guards.

"I don't think there was anybody better than you out there other than Dwayne Wade and Jarvis Hayes," Ford told me. I was shocked. I couldn't believe it. The same thought from before kept flashing through my mind: *I can do this.*

Bill Duffy, one of the top agents in the country, contacted me. It wasn't too long before he had a nickname for me: "Hey Slim Shady, you stood out today. I really like the way you play, you really did a great job," he said.

"You're a blond, white kid that can jump out of the gym, and you're surprising to a lot of people. You're shooting the heck out of it from a distance, and you made 5 of 7 from beyond the NBA arc out there. Amazing."

Duffy's clients included Steve Nash, Yao Ming, and a host of many of the top players in the NBA.

After talking with Danny Ainge, meeting with many other agents, and conversing with Dave Rose and my father, I signed with Duffy. He represented me as my agent, a decision I've never regretted. From Portsmouth, I was invited to the predraft camp in Chicago, another site where NBA scouts gather to look over prospects. We did a lot of drills, lifted weights, ran more drills, and worked out individually for all the NBA teams. For some reason I didn't do as well in Chicago, but I did beat the record for lateral quickness. And I had the memory of Portsmouth to keep me working hard.

When the day came for the NBA draft, I was restless and excited. It was a day I had dreamed of as a kid. The Atlanta Hawks picked me in the second round of that 2003 draft, and I became part of the draft class that included

The 2003–2004 Atlanta Hawks.

number-one pick LeBron James, as well as Carmelo Anthony, Chris Bosh, and Dwayne Wade.

I left Atlanta after one season and signed with Tau, a team in Victoria, Spain. After a year there, I agreed to play for Dynamo in Moscow, Russia, for three years. In 2009 I returned to Spain to play for Real Madrid, and then I returned to Moscow in 2010 to play for Khimki before retiring from basketball.

In all, I played eight years as a professional basketball player, and that journey took me to the far corners of the world. It was fun and a lot of work. The experiences I had changed not only me, but my wife and family.

All this happened, I really believe in my heart, because I set some goals, created a plan to achieve those goals, and then stuck with it.

Set goals for yourself, dare to dream, and put a game plan down on paper.

Jimmer Fredette, who set the college basketball world on fire in 2011, wrote a contract with his brother T.J. when he was in high school. It was a simple contract, reading "I, James T. Fredette, agree on this day, January 27, 2007, to do the work and make the necessary sacrifices to be able to reach my ultimate goal of playing in the NBA."[1] He put the paper above his bed and looked at it every day. He became an NBA lottery pick, the number ten player taken in the 2011 draft after being named the national collegiate player of the year his senior year at BYU.

Remember the common saying, "A goal not written down is only a wish." Wishes don't become reality. Goals do.

Growing up, I had a goal sheet on my bedroom door. My list of goals included a desire to beat Michael Jordan, to make my high school basketball team, to be the best basketball player in the world, to play in the NBA, to get good grades in school, and to serve an LDS mission.

Start young, dream big, create a road map to what you want to be, what you hope to become. Find a hero.

On the basketball court, my hero was Michael Jordan. I patterned my game after his style of play. Off the court, Jesus Christ is the person I decided very early in my life to follow.

I urge everyone to find someone they look up to, someone they want to be like. You can even take positive attributes from many different people and then work hard each day to emulate them, to have those same values and attributes in your life.

When you write down goals on paper, they become visible reminders. But it is just as important to put them in motion by setting a time or deadline by which you want to accomplish them. Don't get stuck. Keep attacking that goal.

Tick, tick, tick. Time is a commodity that is perishable.

I knew my athletic dreams could come true on that day in Portsmouth in 2003. Several months later, the Atlanta Hawks drafted me, and I became an NBA player. This led to many life-changing experiences as my career took me all over the world. Practice had prepared me for this time in my life. But sometimes it isn't all you need.

CHAPTER 4

The Driver

W hen I stepped off the airplane in 2006 at Shereme-
tyevo International Airport in Moscow, Russia, I
knew I'd entered a whole new world.

I'd just signed a contract to play basketball for Dynamo
Moscow, one of the most powerful teams in the European
Basketball League. Moscow, a city of more than ten million people, was intimidating, even with its beautiful
fifteenth-century buildings and their famous cone-shaped,
multicolored, onion-top steeples.

Before that day, my greatest frame of reference for what
Russia would be like came from the 1985 movie *Rocky IV*, in
which Rocky Balboa takes on the gigantic Russian monster
Ivan Drago and wins. I knew Moscow was the capital of a
country that had been an enemy to America during the Cold
War, that this former seat of Soviet communism was home
to the Kremlin, and that President Ronald Reagan had once

With my wife in Russia.

called Russia "the seat of evil." I had heard rumors that the
people were different, unfriendly, even mean, and that the
national pastime was to drink vodka until you passed out.

Dynamo had agreed to pay me to shoot three-pointers
and play lock-down defense. They brought me in to sell
tickets, draw crowds, dunk the ball, and help push the team
to a European championship. As I headed toward the car
that was waiting for me, taking steps toward a new life, I
wondered what I had gotten myself into by signing with this
team in the biggest city in the former Soviet Union.

I had no idea what my life would be like in Moscow.
How would I raise my son, Ryder, and take care of and
protect my wife, LaRee? As an outsider, an American in a

foreign land, I was thousands of miles from my safety net, my friends, and my family back in Orem, Utah.

I felt scared and excited, but mostly, my mind was full of questions about my sanity: Was I crazy? Wasn't it risky to bring my family here? What in the world was I doing?

What I did not know that day I first set foot on Russian soil was that the next few years would change my life. I didn't know that one day Russian president Vladimir Putin would sign papers for the government to issue me a Russian passport and make me an official Russian citizen. And I did not know just how much I'd come to love the Russian people.

I didn't know that I'd learn a valuable lesson about the dangers of pride and self-pity, and an even greater lesson about selflessness. It would be an experience that would transform my family's future, along with the future of thousands of others. Aside from my two-years of service as an LDS missionary to Santiago, Chile, seven years earlier, this visit to this country would kick off the greatest experience of my young life.

I would learn that the Russian people are remarkable human beings who have endured decades of hardships. Russians love their country, and they have dreams for happiness just like Americans. They've had a tough history with oppressive rule by very strong regimes and a broken system. Many Russians over age sixty-five grew up in a time when the wrong kind of glance in the right direction could get them locked up or sent to Siberia. Some of these older people had stood by while family and friends simply disappeared, never to be seen again. Others were forced at gunpoint to join the army, and many of them never returned.

Russians are blunt and straightforward. They don't believe in wasting time; and they get right to the point. Their police and government officials can be easily bribed. Corruption is everywhere. In the months to come, I would see many examples of how things got done in Russia, that with a payoff, you could move past the rule of law. Because of this, trust is tough to come by among Russian people.

But I'm getting way ahead of myself. Let's get back to that first day in Russia. When I got in the car that day at the airport, I took a look at my driver and saw a huge, frowning man with a big belly and gray hair. He looked like he could bite the top off a bottle of vodka, chew the glass, and chug down what was left without blinking an eye. He was *the* stereotypical Russian I had pictured in my mind before I knew any better or more about this people. He pulled up in an old Mercedes sedan that looked like it probably belonged to the Mafia. He glared at me as I got inside and closed the door. He didn't speak English, and I didn't speak Russian. He could have turned the car heater on high, and I'd still have felt colder than a cadaver.

I knew this was not going to work. Not if I wanted to be happy when I traveled by car. And so I asked for a new driver, one who spoke English, at least. And that's how I met Andre—massive, strong, and later dubbed Shrek, after the cartoon character.

Andre was a great guy and ended up being one of my best friends. He took care of me and my family. I trusted him with my kids and my wife, and when we bought a minivan to haul the family around, he took care of it like it was his own. He made sure I paid the right amount of money in restaurants. When we went shopping, he made sure no one cheated or shortchanged us. When we went out, he made sure we landed at the right place—one that was safe. He kept us away from places that were scary or had bad reputations.

Andre would come to the airport, take care of the bags, take care of the kids, and pay the fees for the airport VIP areas. If I had problems with the club or the team, he'd talk to them and act kind of like my agent or representative. The team paid him for his services, and I tipped him well—an amount equal to his salary because I loved him so much. He drove us to church every Sunday and gave my children birthday presents. After four years of working with him every day, I trusted him with my life. I couldn't imagine how different life would be if I'd had to endure life with my first driver.

During my second year in Moscow, I decided to buy a Chrysler Town and Country van. The team had a much nicer car ready for me, but I needed something for the family, so I bought this van with captain chairs, seats for the kids, DVD player—the works. It wasn't a Ferrari, and some of my teammates ribbed me for driving it, but Andre loved it and thought it was the best car in the world. Sometimes he would drive while I'd sit in the back seat and watch movies with the kids.

When I signed to play with Real Madrid and move back to Spain, we decided to sell the van. My wife, LaRee, took off for Spain to get settled, and I took the van to the dealership to sell it for around $22,000. I signed all the papers; but since I had to leave for Spain, I gave Andre permission to finalize the sale. I told him if he could get $25,000 for it, he could keep the difference.

I left for Spain to begin preseason training and called Andre to see if the van had sold. He didn't answer. I naturally got nervous and soon found out that he had driven the van to Ukraine for work and had then sold it for cash and kept it all. I was sad, hurt, disappointed, and shocked to find out that my good friend had cheated me. I loved him, and he loved me and my family.

I didn't understand why he had done this. Was his family suffering enough that he'd cheat me to help them? Had I missed some important clue about his true nature?

I never got an answer from Andre and have failed to contact him many times since. Maybe he thought I owed it to him for all the years of driving me and taking care of me. But in the end, it was dishonest and a sad thing to do, especially to a friend.

As time has passed, this story has brought some interesting questions to mind: Who, exactly, is driving my car? More important, *what* is driving me as a person, as a father, as a husband, as a professional, as a disciple of the Savior? Who is in control of the direction I am headed, and do I trust that person?

Is the driving force in my life something good? Or do I let the forces of evil take over the wheel on occasion?

What about you? When you wake up in the morning, do you have addictions that enslave you, or do you feel free to choose the path you take and the decisions you make because no chains hold you back?

Do the powers that drive you make you happy and bring peace to your heart?

Do those forces make you grateful for blessings in your life?

Do you acknowledge the goodness in others and are you kind to others? Do you serve others and look for ways to ease others' burdens?

Or do you feel a lot of guilt, meet the day with shame, and hide misdeeds and sins? Are you mistrustful, angry, or judgmental? Do you fight with parents and siblings, gossip to friends, cheat, lie, or steal?

There is a real war going on in this world today. There are forces of good and forces of evil. I've seen soldiers of both, and I am a witness to this war.

I see the forces of evil at work when people download music, movies, or software without paying for it, cheating the creators of their rightful royalties and pay. I see this evil as many partake in pornography and allow it to rattle around in their brains and change who they are, even take control of them; an addiction to pornography is as strong and dangerous as any addiction to drugs or alcohol.

On the other side, I see goodness in a group of young people—shovels and rakes in gloved hands—who go to the house of a widow and clean up weeds and leaves. I've walked alongside a missionary companion whose feet are sore, who is hungry and tired but is driven by a desire to teach a lesson from his heart, knowing he's doing God's will by leaving everything in his life behind him as he attends to his calling in a foreign land, speaking a language that is not his own, just so he can testify of Jesus Christ.

President Gordon B. Hinckley said:

That war, so bitter, so intense, has gone on, and it has never ceased. It is the war between truth and error, between agency and compulsion, between the followers of Christ and those who have denied Him. His enemies have used every stratagem in that conflict. They've indulged in lying and deceit. They've employed money and wealth. They've tricked the minds of men. They've murdered and destroyed and engaged in every other unholy and impure practice to thwart the work of Christ. . . .

[Opposition] has been felt in the undying efforts of many, both within and without the Church, to destroy faith, to belittle, to demean, to bear false witness, to tempt and allure and induce our people to practices inconsistent with the teachings and standards of [the] work of God.[1]

The nature of this war is startling, to say the least. But the lessons I have learned are equally powerful and ultimately have the most potential to see me and each of you through the battle to victory. Greatest among these lessons has been the discovery that *who* and *what* drives you through this war define who you are.

And who are you? You are a child of God, created in His image. You are a prince or princess of a righteous and noble King and have a royal promise to inherit all that is His. At baptism, you covenanted to do all you could to be counted with His forces on this earth and in the world to come. Because of this heritage, you have powers beyond measure. You have His name backing you up.

Knowing this about myself has made my choices much easier. I can easily define my heroes and stay clear of the villains who might seek to block the way. I know who the driver is. I am in charge. I cannot—you cannot—allow the car to be driven by others who may let you down. There exists one true pilot and He never crashes.

CHAPTER 5

On Overcoats and Going with the Flow

There are times in your life when you choose who you are and what kind of cover you will wrap yourself in.

This decision is based on many things, such as how you were raised, who your friends are, what challenges you have overcome, and ultimately how comfortable you are with your lifestyle and its compatibility with your core beliefs.

I've made a lot of good choices and a few really bad ones in my life. If you keep reading, you'll find that at least one of those bad choices got me in big, capital-T trouble. But over time, I found out who I wanted to be, how I wanted to live, and what standards I would hold myself accountable to on a daily basis.

Before I reveal that trouble-making exploit, I'd like to tell you a little bit about a well-loved but not-so-fashionable coat I own.

In Russia, it's not just cold, it is freezing, blue-streak

cold. Our basketball team practiced twice a day. Each day, I'd come home in between practices, hang out with the kids, take a nap, and then go back to practice. Wearing a suit to work was both impractical and unnecessary. Instead, I wore my practice uniform—which was basically sweat pants or shorts—and the aforementioned overcoat. Staying warm was one of my top priorities. The overcoat was really long and came down past my knees. It did its job well, and I wore it everywhere, even though it seemed like everyone made fun of me when they saw me in it. They called me the homeless man.

I guess it really was a bit funny and unique that I'd wear an old overcoat, drive a minivan, and hang out at home when I was making a lot of money and could afford something far more fashionable. Other athletes on the team, for example, would wear Gucci leather coats and fancy clothes, go to clubs, act like celebrities, and look the part of high-paid stars every day—even in between practice sessions. They'd pull up to the arena in their luxury cars and get out looking like a million bucks. I'd pull up in my van and get out wearing that overcoat and perhaps looking like I'd just napped under a freeway overpass.

But I was happy and comfortable with myself. And I was warm!

The great British satirist Henry Fielding is known to have said, "Fashion is the science of appearance, and it inspires one with the desire to seem rather than to be." Indeed, trying to look and play a part isn't always a good thing. By the time I played in Russia, the appearance of my long, well-worn overcoat didn't matter much because I had come to believe Fielding's words the hard way as a teenager when I got grounded for an entire year.

Growing up in Orem, Utah, I tried to be a good guy. I thought of myself as a positive, friendly, easygoing person. I was an athlete and I was competitive. Admittedly, there were some who saw my competitive nature as arrogance. But basically I was a normal teenage kid trying to figure out what I wanted to do with my life.

I was very sociable at school and wanted to bring others into my group. Likewise, I also wanted to be accepted. I was somewhat of a jester and tended to joke around a lot. Sometimes my lighthearted, "fun" nature helped lighten the mood or ease my load. For example, one day my mom and dad asked me to mow the lawn. I wanted to impress my mom and goof around a little, so I took the lawn mower and cut the words "I love Mom" in the grass. I didn't care what anybody else thought; I loved my mom and wanted to show her.

Other times, my actions tended to elicit the opposite effect. Like the time I thought it might be funny to scratch the words "Trav is rad" into the passenger side of our car door. But like most people, I felt a great need to be liked, loved, and included. Joking around and "goofing off with friends" helped me feel like I was part of something. But there comes a time when you really need to stop thinking about fitting in—even if it sounds fun and exciting—and think instead about the effect your actions have. This is true at any age.

Let me illustrate with a couple of stories. The first is a personal story of which I'm ashamed, but I want to share it if it helps someone learn something about making good choices.

We are taught that "the natural man is an enemy to God" (Mosiah 3:19), that if we just go with the flow without boundaries we are destined to wander around and get in trouble, that if we don't stand for something, we'll fall for anything.

And in Job we read, "man is born unto trouble, as the sparks fly upward" (Job 5:7).

The key is to avoid trouble and the sparks that come with it. On this occasion, I did not do that.

I was a sophomore in high school, a time when many teens want to make friends, get a driver's license, and be seen in the latest and greatest fashions. I was no different. I sought the approval of the juniors and seniors and really wanted to belong to the group of athletes everyone in school seemed to admire.

Some of the older guys had some cool clothes, just the kind of gear other teens would love to have. A few of my friends learned that these older guys stole this and other clothing from the University Mall and sold what they didn't keep. My friends thought it was a cool thing to do, and somewhere along the line I bought into the idea that it would be a thrill and went along for the ride. (You can see where this is going already, right?)

Walking into the mall, we came up with a plan. Somebody would be the lookout, somebody else would distract the clerk in the store, and another guy would actually steal the stuff. I had a bad feeling about this as soon as we got to the store we'd decided to target. This store also just happened to be the most popular shop in the mall, the place all the cool kids shopped, if you know what I mean. But I had this feeling it was not right, I didn't belong there, and I absolutely shouldn't be a part of it. Everything I'd been taught all my life, and everything I thought I was, screamed at me to run away. I tried to think of excuses, that my mom needed me, or I had a doctor's appointment, anything to get me out of it. I knew stealing was not right. Sadly, I pushed these thoughts away and decided to go along with it.

Two guys went into the dressing room and stuffed clothes under their clothes, while the rest of us played lookout. They made a trip to the car, took the clothes out, returned, and did it again. They came back for their third load. Things started getting rushed and more chaotic. In another dressing room, two other guys started stuffing my clothes with clothes. When I came out of that dressing room, the clerk took one look at us and said she was calling the cops.

I froze. For a split second a voice inside me said, "Run! Run! Run!" But I froze. I was scared to death. My friend started walking fast, but the clerk grabbed him and then grabbed me. I almost wet my pants. The police came and took us both to a room in the back of the store and began asking us questions. They asked me my name and I told them I was Frank-something. They said that had better be my real name or I'd be in even more trouble. They knew that wasn't my name because I wasn't the first kid who had tried that on them. I knew I was lying, but my friends were telling me to stay strong and keep faking my real identity.

I couldn't do it.

The police took me outside, separate from my friends, and as I was walking to the police car in handcuffs I passed by a member of my ward whom I knew very well. I tried to hide my handcuffs and act like nothing was up; but there was Brother Lyman, and I couldn't hide. He saw me. I was embarrassed and humiliated.

I was taken to the police station, where my dad came to pick me up and judgment day ensued. I felt awful. What had I done? Why had I done this? I ended up with a parole officer, had to do community service, and was grounded for an entire year. My mom was livid. She later drove me to the mall and made me walk in by myself and apologize to the store manager.

"I'm sorry for what I did to you and your store," I said.

The manager appreciated that I came to see him but he had a warning for me. He said, "It was brave of you to come in and I hope you learned your lesson. It is wrong to steal things. I can't let you come into this store again, not for at least six months."

I agreed.

This event should never have happened. I was embarrassed, and I lost respect from those who loved me. My mother's words cut deep: "I have spent my whole life teaching about choices. I hope that you will understand the tremendous effect of your decisions, not just on you but everyone around you."

I'd been taught all my life to be honest with myself, others, and the Lord. I'd been taught not to rationalize and that lying and stealing were wrong; but I chose not to live what I'd been taught.

None of this would ever have happened if I had made a pledge to myself to be honest long before this experience. When the temptation came and the pressure from my friends mounted, I should have said no and walked away. The best advice I can give is to make up your mind about how you will act way before anything tempts you, and then act on that promise to yourself.

If you don't have a plan, you are destined to fail. The greatest benefit of directing your energies in a planned direction is that many of your choices will be made beforehand. When you get to a tough spot or are tempted to do something wrong, you will have already made a choice as to how you will handle it because you have identified a plan of action.

Successful people avoid compromising situations. They don't run and hide and make a situation worse. They take responsibility for their actions and use mistakes to improve and learn.

You cannot cheat your way to being a good person. When you cheat, it hurts you spiritually and takes away from your self-esteem. Also, cheaters usually get caught.

In my second season playing for Dynamo in Moscow, Russia, we were in the playoffs for the Russian championship. All season long it had appeared that we weren't getting good calls during games. I know almost every basketball team in the world and their fans feel like they don't get the breaks in officiating, but this appeared to be a pattern for us. When Dynamo played, weird stuff happened with the officials.

In the playoffs we met a team called Triumph. They had paid off the referees with a lot of money, and word around the league was that this happened quite frequently with some officials.

In the game with Triumph, it all boiled down to the final seconds of the game. We had the ball out of bounds under the opposing team's basket with just under three seconds to play. We passed the ball the length of the court. I caught it and passed it to Henry Domercant, who was the leading scorer in the NCAA when he was in America. Domercant shot the ball, had it blocked, caught the ball, and shot it again from behind the backboard. It went in, and we were ahead by two points.

We celebrated hard because we thought the game was over. It was a buzzer beater, and the clock read zero. But the refs came over to us and said there was 1 second left in the game. That was impossible because we started the winning play at the opposite end of the court with 2.6 seconds on the clock. No way could we have made two passes and had Domercant's two shots in less than 2.6 seconds.

Crazy. It was nuttier than an acorn factory, and we couldn't believe it.

The officials gave Triumph the ball at half court and put a second on the clock. They threw the ball inbounds, and the guy who caught it dribbled once and faked a shot as our defender flew by him. He then gathered himself and shot the ball. It went in from beyond the three-point line. Triumph won the game.

We heard the Triumph coach tell his players to run to the locker room and get off the court so nobody could refute the basket or the clock. The owner of my team was a high ranking member of the KGB and a personal friend of Russian President Vladimir Putin. He was furious. I decided to get off the court because I thought there might be a riot in the stands and on the floor.

About twenty-four hours later, we arrived home and our coach called a team meeting for the next day. The Russian Federation reviewed films of the game and found the scorekeeper at the officials table did not start the clock on time. He was fined $10,000 for his actions. Two of the three officials had been paid an undisclosed amount of money to make sure Triumph won. The scorekeeper was banned for six months, one of the referees was banned for three years, and the head referee was banned for life for setting up the arrangement.

All these decisions and disclosures made us happy; but instead of giving us the win, the Federation ordered us to play the entire game all over again. We did and won by twenty points. That game advanced us to the Russian championship game against CSKA, but we lost that game.

The next year, the Federation put microphones in the locker rooms where the officials dressed and discovered a huge conspiracy, not just with these refs but with a larger, very tainted circle of officials.

Cheating refs? Why? Greed and a desire to go with the flow—the same two things I grappled with the day I decided it was more important to steal and fit in than do the right thing and be rejected; the very things that you avoid if you know who you are, who your driver is, and what your plan is.

In basketball, we create a game plan. The game plan is based on scouting reports about the strengths and weaknesses of an opponent and outlines how to attack both. A game plan has every detail covered. If you are guarding a dribbler who favors his right hand and likes to go to that side, you adjust your defense to not worry so much about him going to his left.

In life, your game plan might include reading the scriptures; praying every day; and avoiding drinking, doing drugs, and other inappropriate activities. Your plan might include a goal to do something physical every day to help your body grow and be healthy. The "For the Strength of Youth" pamphlet, available to all LDS youth, has a great game plan on how to attack issues of modesty, chastity, and media exposure, as well as how to prepare for missions and marriage.

Once you have a plan, you will feel more confident in your own skin. Once you start meeting your goals and experiencing success, your feelings of self-worth will grow and your self-esteem will increase. When you accomplish things, you will feel better about yourself.

If you know yourself, your strengths and weaknesses, and have a game plan to avoid your weaknesses and rely on your strengths, it won't bother you when people tease you or make fun of you for wearing an old, long coat. In fact, you are likely to find yourself warmer, humbler, and safer than those who choose instead to go with the flow and fit in with the crowd.

CHAPTER 6

Saying Good-Bye
to Mom

Friends used to tease me because I loved my mother so much.

Scratch that. I didn't just love her, I worshipped and adored her. She was my best friend. Abraham Lincoln once said of his mother, "All that I am, all that I hope to be, I owe to my angel mother."[1] I've been able to relate to that quote my entire life, and I've always believed it. If it weren't for my mother, I wouldn't be here. She brought me into this world. And she taught me many valuable lessons.

Lincoln's last words from his mother were: "Be something, Abe."[2]

Those are interesting words. His mother didn't say, "Be someone." She said, "Be something, Abe." There is a significant difference. *Someone* can refer to any unspecified person; but I think of *something* as a person or thing of importance.

My mom was always very encouraging. She, like most

parents, told me I could be whatever I wanted to be and I could accomplish anything I set my mind to.

In the fall of 1996, my older brother, Tyler, was serving a mission in Japan and my younger brother, Landon, was just fourteen. My twin sisters, Heather and Hollie, were in elementary school in Orem, Utah. My father was the bishop of a singles ward. Our lives seemed normal, busy, and happy. And then one day I overheard my dad and mom talking about how my mom's back ached and how she was in a lot of pain. She had visited many doctors and experts trying to figure out the reason behind the pain. After months with no definite answer, she decided to take the advice of a specialist and go in for a procedure to find what was going on.

On January 14, 1997, Dr. Doug Kohler came out of the operating room of the Utah Valley Hospital having diagnosed my mother with cancer. They later found that the cancer had spread all over her back and in her organs, including her pancreas. They told her she had two weeks to live and there was nothing they could do for her but make her comfortable.

My mother came out of the anesthesia and learned she had cancer by overhearing the doctors and my father talking in her hospital room. My father rushed to her side to comfort her. She instantly was concerned for her children.

My father recalls that her first words were, "I am glad it is me and not one of our kids."

Hours later they called my siblings and me to the hospital to break the news to us.

I was in shock. It was devastating. You never talk about what you would do if you lost your mother. It breaks your heart and affects you in a way you cannot explain. Life stopped. I felt empty, lost, and without emotion.

My son Mason acts like me but looks like his mother. He acts like I did around my mother. He is a pleaser and loves to be helpful. When my mom said she couldn't find something, boom, I was after it, looking everywhere for what she was missing. If she was watching TV and said she wished she had some popcorn, boom, I was in the kitchen making the popcorn and then bringing it to her in our big silver bowl. She loved cottage cheese and tomatoes with a little salt and pepper sprinkled on top. Sometimes I'd make it for her just to please her. It was great to see her smile and enjoy it.

I was very close to my mother. I adored her and always wanted to be around her. She was a jokester, like me. She was always nice and respectful to others and she was compassionate and fun. Every good value in life, she had. Our personalities were in line with each other. We thought the same thoughts, it seemed. It was very hard to watch the nurses come in and give her morphine patches and see the room fill up with medical equipment. It was hard to see her feet swell up and her body essentially begin to waste away and die. I will never get those images out of my mind. It was heartbreaking to watch someone I would give up my life for and protect from anything suffer so much.

When she was sick, I spent many nights at her side, rubbing her arms and legs to ease the pain that gravitated there.

She slowly became gaunt and weak and slept more and more as doctors gave her more drugs for pain.

Journal entry

March 26, 1997

Today is one of the worst days of my life. My mom has pancreatic cancer and only has a few more days to live. I am by her side at the moment. She is so beautiful, and I love her and always will. Oh Mommy, why do you have to go? I wish and pray that she wouldn't die but I see her in all the pain and I crumble. I know it is her time. It hurts me inside to see how weak she is. Oh Mom, you are the most perfect mom in the world! Last night I was laying by her side and she said, "Go on a mission. Promise me you will go." I have to go! I would do anything for you, I would trade places with you in a second just so you could live one more day. Mom, I just don't know how to tell you how much I love you and how special you are. I will love you always and forever!

The previous fall, everything was fine and I had a healthy mom. Two days after I wrote the preceding journal entry, she was gone from this world.

I always appreciated my mom's unique ability to love others regardless of their strengths or weaknesses. She made others feel very comfortable in our home. Her amazing testimony of the gospel and her strong faith in God were exemplified in every aspect of her life. She loved the Church, and she loved my dad. She was the perfect example of someone enduring to the end.

Her favorite scripture was about charity:

> Wherefore, if a man have faith he must needs have hope; for without faith there cannot be any hope.
>
> And again, behold I say unto you that he cannot have faith and hope, save he shall be meek, and lowly of heart.
>
> If so, his faith and hope is vain, for none is acceptable before God, save the meek and lowly in heart; and if a man be meek and lowly in heart, and confesses by the power of the Holy Ghost that Jesus is the Christ, he must needs have charity; for if he have not charity he is nothing; wherefore he must needs have charity.
>
> And charity suffereth long, and is kind, and envieth not, and is not puffed up, seeketh not her own, is not easily provoked, thinketh no evil, and rejoiceth not in iniquity but rejoiceth in the truth, beareth all things, believeth all things, hopeth all things, endureth all things.
>
> Wherefore, my beloved brethren, if ye have not charity, ye are nothing, for charity never faileth. Wherefore, cleave unto charity, which is the greatest of all, for all things must fail. . . .

Wherefore, my beloved brethren, pray unto the Father all with the energy of heart, that ye may be filled with this love, which he hath bestowed upon all who are true followers of his Son, Jesus Christ; that ye may become the sons of God; that when he shall appear we shall be like him, for we shall see him as he is; that we may have this hope; that we may be purified even as he is pure. Amen. (Moroni 7:42–46, 48)

Because of my mom's love for them, these verses are the ones I have read the most in my life.

I remember being at basketball practice at Utah Valley State College. Coach Jeff Reinert was in the process of breaking down video and was getting after our team for not playing hard as he pointed out mistakes on the film.

"You guys don't have pressure on you," Reinert said. "Travis is the only one with pressure on him because his mom has cancer."

I ran out of the room and tears filled my eyes. It was the first time anyone from outside my family had made a public declaration that my mom had cancer. The words hung in the air like a ton of bricks ready to fall. Reinert came out of the room and consoled me. I missed practice that day and a few more after that. The funeral was brutal, but all of my teammates and coaches came, and I appreciated them being there to support me.

While it was extremely difficult to see my mother die,

it was also a great comfort to know of and believe in the Atonement and resurrection. It helps so much to know I will have the privilege of seeing her again. It's comforting to know that her beautiful face will be brought back to perfection and her arms will be warm and strong when she hugs me again.

I know my mother's death was not the end of all that she is, that she is living with her mom and family and friends who have also gone on. I know she is doing good things and she's looking after us when the Lord allows her to. I believe that she had simply finished her work on the earth and continues sacred work on the other side of the veil.

I want to talk to her; I want her to see my two sons and my daughter. I wanted her to be there when I opened my mission call and when I returned home from serving. I wish she could have been there on senior night at BYU when other parents stood with the senior basketball players for their final home game. I wish she could have been there for my marriage to meet my beautiful wife, LaRee, and attend the sealing of our daughter, Halle, to us with our two boys. But she wasn't there physically.

When I was drafted in the NBA, I would have given anything to have her there, to have her hug me and tell me how proud she was of me.

Days before she died, I knelt at her bedside when she looked at me and asked that I serve a mission. I had always wanted to go on a mission; but as I began playing basketball in college, I had sometimes wondered if I would be able to set aside my athletic career and scholarship.

At that moment I promised my mother I would go on a mission. The only certain thing I had to do after that was keep my promise.

CHAPTER 7

Pay Back:
Go, Serve, Grow

L ooking at a sunset, drinking in its beauty, feeling the sun shine on your face and the wind as it blows through your hair—these are gifts to us, proof that we are alive and God loves us.

Likewise, dunking a basketball, making a three-point shot at the buzzer, taking a wet brush to a blank canvass, turning notes on a page into a beautiful melody, teaching children to recognize sounds and words, and so many other talents are also gifts, reminders that God blesses each of us with unique talents and abilities.

But greater than these gifts are those that come to us with and through the Atonement of the Savior, Jesus Christ: Knowledge that if we mess up, we can receive forgiveness and have another chance. Knowledge that after death, we can live again. Knowledge that we are children of a living God.

This knowledge is worth sharing. It's a message worth shouting out to the world. Countless numbers of God's children are hungry for the gospel message, for the knowledge I had been so freely given as a youth in Orem, Utah, supported and loved by parents who knew that message to be true. After my mother's death, sharing that message became a way to thank her for the gifts she had given me by teaching me the gospel.

My mission was payback.

The decision to serve was one I had thought about when I was very young. I wanted to be a missionary. I was going to be a missionary! But, as so often happens in life, there were times I became distracted and lost focus on that goal.

I was really good at basketball, and there were scholarship offers waiting for me—ones that might evaporate if I put school on hold. I wondered if going away for two years might hurt my chances or potential to become a professional basketball player. I could go for two years and my body could break down, I could become weak, my timing and my shot could suffer. It could take another few years to get my skills back.

It was 1997, and I was eighteen with my entire life ahead of me. Did I really want to leave for two years?

Shortly after my mom died, I drove my Toyota truck to the cemetery, pulled alongside her grave, and sat there listening to music. I just wanted to be close to her, and I thought this would be as good a way as any to do that. I was so sad; I was lost at the time. I didn't know what my next step would be. I turned off my truck, and the music died. My words came slowly in a prayer. I asked my Heavenly Father what I should do. I asked Him to look after my mother and let her know how much I loved her.

An incredible spirit surrounded me in that truck. I felt a message hit me in the heart like a spear. It was a message to be strong, to go on a mission, and to know that my family would be watched over in my absence; serving a mission was the right thing. I decided then and there I would do everything I could to go on a mission. I met with Bishop Bernie Lancaster and filled out my papers.

It was the best decision I ever made.

For me, it didn't matter where I would be called to serve. I felt a deep, profound desire to do what was right and serve no matter where or how hard the call. My older brother and my dad had served in Japan, and I thought maybe that's where I was destined to go.

When I opened up my mission call, the letter said Santiago, Chile, and I was happy and thrilled to learn about the country and speak Spanish. Chile is a ribbon-like country that borders the Pacific Ocean and is one of the most stable and prosperous countries in South America.

When I arrived in Chile, I was taken to the mission home where I received an orientation about the mission rules, took a shower, met my trainer, and was sent off with Elder Jason Abbott from Las Vegas.

Two hours from the mission home we were on a bus packed with Chileans. Elder Abbott said, "OK, Elder

Official missionary name tag.

Hansen, I'm going to give you some tasks, and one of the first is to get up and teach your first lesson."

Now, I admit this was a scary thing to do. I was so nervous my hands were dripping sweat. I pulled out a card that showed John the Baptist performing the baptism of Jesus.

"I'm a missionary representing The Church of Jesus Christ of Latter-day Saints," I said with a loud voice.

The bus was loud and the diesel engine was even louder.

"If you haven't been baptized like this, you need to talk to us. I know Jesus Christ is the Savior. If you are baptized like this, you will follow His example and He will bless you."

I gave a lesson on baptism by immersion to the captive audience on that noisy bus. When I sat down I was shaking. I had a case of butterflies doing the cha-cha in my stomach. It was very intimidating and I was really afraid, but when I stood up and did it, the fear left me. It was a phenomenal experience. That first day in Chile I learned to face my fears, to be proud of why I was there and what I needed to accomplish. I knew I was there to baptize, to bring people to Christ.

The mission home had been in a nice, wealthy area of Santiago. My first apartment was in Ochagavia, a poor district in the middle of Santiago. When we pulled up in front of our apartment, I saw a shack as large as a big bedroom in America. Our *mamita* lived in the front of the shack and we lived in the back. Our *mamita* was a member of the Church, but she was inactive. She was a wonderful human being, kind and compassionate. She did all of our laundry and cooked for us, and all we had to do was give her a hug and a kiss on the cheek. In this small room, I had a stool to sit my scriptures on and I slept in a bunk bed. It was humble and nothing much to speak of. But it was there that I forged a love for the work, for my Savior, and for the people of that country.

On April 25, 1999, an estimated crowd of 57,500 Church members gathered for a regional conference. I was seated along with my missionary companion in a massive soccer stadium to hear from President Gordon B. Hinckley.

What we witnessed was a miracle. Members gathered from the Santiago region and from cities throughout the nation as they traveled for this unique opportunity to hear from a prophet of God. "I can scarcely believe what I see," said President Hinckley as he looked out at the crowded stadium. "I have trouble holding back the tears. I feel so profoundly grateful for your presence, for the great effort you have made to be here, for your sacrifice in coming, for your willingness to sit here in the cold. May the Lord bless you because of your love for Him."[1]

I remember waking up that cold morning to attend the conference and rushing to get my white shirt and tie on before taking the long bus trip into Santiago. I remember that Chile had been experiencing a severe drought, and many members and missionaries had been fasting and praying that when the prophet came, he would bring with him rain.

The Spirit was strong as we listened intently to Elder Russell M. Nelson and President Hinckley that Saturday morning. During his talk, President Hinckley spoke of a drought thirty years earlier, in 1969, that had swept over the country of Chile. He said, "I remember that occasion 30 years ago this April. I remember the plea for rain and I remember the reports that rain fell upon the land. That was not my doing. That was the work of God our Eternal Father in behalf of the people of this land. I believe it was an answer to the faith and the prayers of the Latter-day Saints, then few in number, whose very faith came to bless the entire nation.

"I want to say to every one of you that if you will live the gospel, if you will live in faith, if you will do what you ought to do, not only will you be blessed, but this entire people will be blessed because the God of heaven will smile upon you with love for you and for the land of which you are a part."[2]

As he ended his talk, President Hinckley said, "Now, it

CONFERENCIA ESPECIAL

SESIÓN GENERAL

HIMNOS

"Te damos Señor
nuestras gracias,
que mandas de
nuevo venir,
profetas con tu
evangelio..."

25 DE ABRIL DE 1999

can rain." We then sang the precious, inspiring hymn "God Be with You Till We Meet Again."[3]

By the time the final prayer was offered, I had drops of rain hitting my suit jacket. By the time we walked out of the stadium and onto our assigned bus, it was pouring. It continued to rain for days after that meeting.

This amazing story spread, and within the next few weeks and months, church attendance skyrocketed, baptisms soared to an all-time high, and I had witnessed a miracle.

During that meeting more than a decade ago, President Hinckley also spoke of a slogan that hung on a banner from the stadium. It read, "Just Do It." He talked of the principle of tithing and how faith needs to replace doubt. When he referred to the law of tithing, he said when keeping the commandments and other important principles of the gospel, to "Just do it," like that huge Nike banner proclaimed: no excuses, just do it.

I believe that to be the best simple counsel I have ever heard. It certainly applies to preparation for a mission. "If you know these things, happy are ye if ye do them" (John 13:17).

In the blessing I received when I was set apart as a missionary, I was counseled to be obedient and be aware of the promises found in Doctrine and Covenants section four. I was admonished to work diligently, learn from the people I worked with, let my personality shine forth, always be filled with love and happiness, and give my heart to no other person but the Lord. I was told if I would rise early and work hard, strength and good health would be mine.

My mission was one of the top baptizing missions in the Church. I baptized eleven people the first week I was there. We taught people on beaches, on the streets, and on buses. Almost everyone would let us in their house to talk. It was wonderful.

However, I know in many other missions it's not as easy to find and teach that many people so quickly. Many missionaries may go two years and get in the baptismal font but a few times, if any.

Missions are not easy. There are times when every missionary feels helpless and discouraged. But when you feel like giving up, that is exactly the time you need to know how to find strength and be guided by the Spirit.

In many ways, playing basketball was great preparation for my mission. It taught me the importance of practice, working with teammates, taking instruction from coaches, dealing with adversity, knowing what to do when I feel like quitting, and how to overcome challenges on and off the court. I know not all young men and women have the opportunity to learn what I did from basketball, but you can take experiences from other things and have them apply in the same way.

Here are five suggestions that might help in preparing for a mission.

1. **Cultivate experiences with the Spirit in your life.** Find a way to experience the Holy Ghost, to recognize His

influence, feel His promptings, and understand how the Spirit operates. The thoughts that come from the Holy Ghost are different than those that come from Satan. You need to be able to feel the Holy Ghost, trust Him, and know who He is so He can guide you.

2. **Practice living right.** If you do not discipline yourself to obey rules, commandments, and guidelines before a mission, you will struggle to do so as a missionary. In basketball, if you don't practice dribbling, in a game, you can easily have the ball stolen or lose control of it. It's the same thing in life. Learn to pray and listen for answers. Prayer is a fundamental action of those who seek God and desire to teach His word.

3. **Learn everything you can.** Don't wait for a mission to study the gospel and learn about the plan of salvation, the Atonement, forgiveness, faith, and the history of the Restoration. Start now, today; decide this moment that you will be prepared. Go to seminary, listen to instructors, take notes, start a journal, mark your scriptures. Knowledge is power. Study as many topics as you can in school, ask experts questions, and find answers.

4. **Experience life.** You need as many life experiences as you can get to help you grow and relate to others. Go kayaking, climb a mountain, read good books, work for somebody, earn a paycheck, save money, gather fast offerings, visit

Scan this QR code (or visit http://youtu.be/M0sGIb 3Ehcg) to hear Travis testify of the importance of keeping a journal.

the sick and needy, become an expert at doing chores. On a mission, you work hard. You meet people and you need to be able to talk to them. Some do this easily, others coast by, some fight against it. Don't waste opportunities.

5. **Apply yourself.** If you have a job, do it well. I'm still mad at myself for not applying myself every day of my life before my mission. I missed out on meeting and making more friends in high school. I should have been talking to a lot more people and making many more friends. I wish I had. Find your strengths and use them; discover your weaknesses and conquer them.

My mission president, Rollie Walker, from Idaho Falls, Idaho, is one of the most remarkable men I have ever known. He told us, "If you will do for two years what most won't, you'll be able to do what most can't the rest of your life."

This is a quote I have found to be true. There is a hero inside all of us, waiting to use the gifts we have been blessed with, waiting to do more, not just for two years but for the rest of our lives.

CHAPTER 8

The Badge

Being drafted to play in the NBA opens all kinds of doors in terms of celebrity, financial gains, and negotiations for future contracts as an athlete.

The same type of thing happens when a person becomes an Eagle Scout, serves a full-time mission, or earns a college degree.

These badges are important and worthwhile. If you seek them, they will pay significant dividends in your life.

Let's take the NBA badge, for instance.

An athlete who is drafted to the NBA represents hundreds of hours of work by professional scouts researching every aspect of his life. These experts break down film, talk to coaches, watch you play in person, and size up how you do against other athletes. You are measured, poked at, weighed, timed, probed, tested, and examined by doctors.

When an NBA team decides to draft you in the first or

second round, it is a great honor because it means you have been judged to possess a certain degree of talent and you are counted among the best basketball players in the world.

When Atlanta drafted me, it changed my financial future. I played one year of a two-year contract with Atlanta before deciding to leave. The situation was simply not right for me to find playing time and develop my skills at the next level. My agent worked out a contract for me to play with Tau in Spain. I saw firsthand just how important the NBA badge was when I made this move.

Having the badge was like being able to go through passport lines with a diplomatic stamp. If you go to Europe and you have played in the NBA, you have a tremendous amount of credibility. The European owners, coaches, media, and fans really believe in and respect the scouts who work in the NBA. Because they believe the NBA experts know talent, they also believe that any player in the NBA must be very, very good—even if that player doesn't actually play very well.

I learned this from firsthand experience. My first year in Tau, I definitely didn't play well; but I didn't get cut because I was an NBA player. I had hurt my back and I played particularly poorly in January 2005. The media wanted to know what was wrong, so they called a press conference to ask me.

"Why do you play so badly? Why are you struggling?"

"Porque soy malo," I told them, which in Spanish means "Because I am bad."

They all laughed and thought I was being funny. "You can't be bad," they replied. "You played in the NBA."

But I was being truthful. When they finally understood I was being honest with them and that I really was struggling, they respected that and cheered me on.

But it was brutal there in Spain. European basketball is very tactical and deliberate. It's physical and demanding. My coach was a tough, gruff-mannered Serbian named Dusko Ivanovic. As a player, he had developed the reputation of being hard as nails. It was said that after he practiced for eight hours a day, he'd go run stairs in stadiums. Imposing at six foot seven, he could yell and make the bark fall off a tree.

As a coach, he was often downright mean. We used to say he wasn't even human because he was so extremely demanding. He seemed to love to punish players physically with drills and exercises. In the NBA, I had practiced for an hour every day. In the Euroleague, I practiced twice a day every day and even practiced on Christmas. In preseason, we'd practice three times a day.

One thing Ivanovic liked to do was take his players outside to run over uneven fields filled with rocks. He believed the uncertainty of the landing area on an uneven surface would make our ankles stronger so we would avoid ankle sprains. But all it did was weaken me and took the life right out of my basketball game.

Ivanovic wore me right out. I couldn't move and I couldn't play. One day I worked so hard I blew out my calf muscle. The back of my lower leg was so black it looked like someone had beaten it with a baseball bat. The torn muscles inside were bleeding, and I was hobbled.

Ivanovic also liked to fine players, and he found ways to discipline me and thus take my money. Disagreeing or arguing with him was always followed by a fine. Many of my teammates joked that if you looked at him wrong, he would fine you. He chose what we ate and wore and where we could go and what we could do every day. In the beginning I got mad at him for this and let it show in the way I played.

As I mentioned, I was broken. Even the badge of being an NBA player wasn't helping in this situation.

But then I chose to wear a different badge. This other badge was one most missionaries are very familiar with. I decided I would not let him get to me or distract me from becoming the player I wanted to be. I chose to build a force field around me, to not allow him to affect the way I played. After this, I excelled and began to have great games. Once I decided to take the high road and not buck his system or play his game, I was happier and a stronger man. It was a tough, tough time. But I'm proud that I survived. I later learned I was one of the few American players to have gone over there and worked with Ivanovic and stuck it out on his team. Because I didn't give up, he tried to re-sign me every year after I left, but I was ready to move on.

Another thing that helped me in Spain was the fact that I spoke their language and I was loyal to the club. I chose to make a real effort to get along with my teammates and

Playing in Victoria, Spain.

the media and built good relationships with the trainers. Obviously, this habit is a good one no matter what you do.

In late January, after I'd had my interview with the press and admitted I was playing poorly, the team played an important game in the Copa Del Rey play-off tournament. Things changed for me that game. I played really well, and we were able to go to the first Final Four in the history of the club. In fact, both years I played for Tau in Victoria, Spain, we went to the Final Four, and every time I'd shoot, the fans would call me *El Mormón*.

I made it in Spain, and eventually in Russia, then back to Spain and Russia again because I had the NBA badge and I backed it up with the badge I had earned as a missionary—a badge that represented hard work and an attitude people appreciated. Many experiences I had on my mission in Chile

66

paved the way for me later in life. They are skills I still use today.

If you give up two years of your life to serve God and pay back what has been given to you, you will be rewarded with an education you cannot acquire in any other way. Very few people, at any other time in their lives, can live, study, and teach the great truths of Jesus Christ 24/7 like missionaries can for two years.

Here are a few examples of skills you can develop in two years on a mission:

Communication. You learn to talk to people, mostly to total strangers. You grow in confidence in being able to express yourself. You also learn to take criticism from somebody besides your parents.

Overcoming fear. You learn how to overcome fear, which can be a stumbling block throughout your life in dealing with issues, challenges, and setbacks. Overcoming fear allows you to move forward and avoid the paralyzing effect of being idle.

Diplomacy. You gain an understanding of what it takes to live with a total stranger—your new companion. You play the give-and-take game, laugh and cry together, and handle adversity as a team. What greater training can you gain for a job, career, or marriage?

Leadership. Corporations pay thousands of dollars to train employees how to lead, set goals, achieve, and grow. A mission does all those things automatically every day. You are given opportunities to speak, express yourself, take charge of a meeting, plan and map out a strategy, and make tough decisions. You learn how to bring an investigator from point A to point B and how to get Church members involved and strengthen their faith.

Humility. One of the greatest traits you can acquire in life is humility. To be taught by somebody your own age who may not be as talented or as smart as you are, to get along with others who may not have your same interests, to recognize there is something greater than yourself, and to appreciate the poor and destitute can all help you gain humility.

Accountability. The great universities of the world hand out grades and degrees. On a mission, you learn how to measure up to your goals daily and make progress. You report to yourself, your companion, your district or zone leader, your mission president, and most important, to the Lord. Your mission president isn't there to babysit you every day. You have to push yourself to get out of bed, study, learn, teach, and find.

Scripture scholarship. Schools of theology hand out degrees in religion. With extensive daily study of the scriptures for two years, you obtain a remarkable reservoir of knowledge about God and gospel principles. You learn to train your mind and memory. It is a wonderful feeling that helps your self-esteem. There is nothing better than to wake up in the middle of nowhere, with a garden hose for a shower and a bunk bed full of fleas, and study the scriptures with your companion. Until you do it, until you experience it, you can't explain it. It is a remarkable experience that changes your life.

Gratitude. No matter the area, most missionaries tend to come into contact with the meek and poor of the earth more frequently than any other category of people. Having poor families give up a week's wages to feed you because they love you can be a real life-changer. It taught me to never take for granted what I have at home again. Seeing how happy people can be who have nothing helped me discover what I really need in life, as opposed to what I want.

Productivity. If you ever want to see time fly and the days just melt away, a mission gives you the perfect opportunity. I truly learned what it means to be productive, to accomplish a lot in just a little time. A mission helps you learn to avoid wasting time and to discipline yourself to make every minute count.

These are only a few of the educational rewards of missionary service. The benefits are priceless, if you take it seriously and apply yourself.

CHAPTER 9

Quitters Never Win

Three times in my career I wanted to pack it in and quit. Discouragement and disappointment can be poison to the soul, and it takes a lot of hard work, prayer, and encouragement from those you love to make things work.

You cannot succeed if you quit. You may learn from the experience and get better; but if you walk away from a worthy task, goal, or assignment, you might as well cross it off, because you let it get away and you lost.

The first time I almost quit?

My first year at BYU. I had just married LaRee, and practices were extremely tough under skills-development coach and defensive coordinator Heath Schroyer. Coach Schroyer came to BYU with Steve Cleveland from Fresno Community College in 1997 and he has a reputation for motivating players and pushing them. It is a reputation that got him a job as head coach for both Portland State and

Wyoming, and later a stint on the staff of UNLV in Las Vegas.

I joined teammates Garner Meads, Jesse Pinegar, and Shaun Opunui as rookies to be trained, tested, and molded into shape by Schroyer. The work with Schroyer served many purposes. Part of it was to get us acclimated to conditioning as Division I athletes, but some of it may have been to simply see if we could hack it and weed out those who couldn't.

Schroyer would keep us after practice and we'd divide up and go three against three or five-on-five. The idea was to get three defensive stops in a row where the other guys did not score.

We'd knock knees, claw at each other, race to close out shooters, bang each other around, push, shove, chase, and get two stops in a row, and then that darned walk-on—Dane Runia, son of former BYU star Scott Runia—would knock down a crazy corner three-point shot. Schroyer would say the dreaded words, "Start over at zero," and it would begin all over again. It is hard to get three stops in a row.

I'd go home with blisters on my feet, and the skin on my soles was peeling off. Soaking them in Epsom salts brought some relief, and every night I'd try to regain some of my strength to play again the next day. Schroyer was really hard on us, and my confidence was at an all-time low. I began to think it wasn't worth it—all the time away from my wife, away from school, and away from my family. I wanted to be done.

It got to the point where I told LaRee, "I don't need this. I'll just go to school and get a job."

"No way are you going to quit," she said. "You gave your word, you said you'd do it. Stick with it. Keep playing."

I hadn't been home from my mission to Chile for too long, and my legs were still slowly coming back. I could blow past everybody the first few minutes of practice, but then I'd slow down. It took the better part of a year of practicing every day and going through huge physical and mental challenges before I got to the point where I felt like basketball was what I really wanted to do, and I was committed again.

My wife was a great inspiration to me. She encouraged me to look at things in a different way. When I had a difficult day with a coach or another player, she'd tell me, "Don't let one coach or one person or one practice kill your dream."

In time, I finished my BYU career with all-league honors twice and was named the Mountain West Conference defensive player of the year as a senior. The teams I played on at BYU became the foundation for the most successful run of winning seasons in school history.

The second time I wanted to quit basketball came in 2004, my first season with the Atlanta Hawks, when I got a stress fracture in my foot and was out for a few months. I was discouraged. Living the lifestyle of an active member of the Church is not easy in the NBA. Opportunities for temptation and distraction abound. And not joining the crowd can sometimes mean isolation. Coupled with team politics, poor trades, and a lot of egos, the situation had reached a boiling point for me.

This was all too hard. I wasn't getting the playing minutes I thought I deserved, and all I could think about was myself and how I didn't fit in. I didn't want to be there anymore. I wasn't getting the ball. I wasn't close to any of my teammates. I wanted to be done and thought there were many other things I could do with my life.

Once more, LaRee came to the rescue. "You are not quitting," she said. "You are going to stick with it and you are going to persevere and you are going to come out a bigger man because of this. If you stick with it, good things will happen." She was right.

The third time I wanted to quit was after I left Atlanta and signed with Tau in Victoria, Spain. My agent had warned me about Coach Ivanovic—you know, the guy from the last chapter who made it his goal to make life miserable. I wondered how hard Ivanovic could be. After all, I'd been with Coach Schroyer, and I knew guys who had been coached by Rick Majerus at the University of Utah. Majerus was notorious for his tough manner. I thought I knew how hard it could be.

I had no idea.

The pre-season at Tau was crazy. In addition to practicing three times a day, there were strict routines that we had to follow. For lunch, everyone on the team had to sit at the table wearing a Tau polo shirt and eat the same buffet every day. Day in and day out we ate a salad made with corn, onions, eggs, tomatoes, oil and vinegar, and then they served chicken and pasta with either white or red sauce, yogurt with bananas, and water. Every day.

We were not given permission to leave the table until everyone was finished eating, and then we were allowed to go to our rooms and take a nap, shower, or prepare. Ivanovic scheduled every minute of every day. We joked that we even had to schedule when we could to go to the bathroom.

In preseason, they bussed us up in the northern mountains of Spain. There was nothing there but mountains, a gym, and workouts three times a day. We ran for an hour every day. It wasn't just a jog, it was a sprint, and we were timed.

So, there I was in the middle of the mountains doing this run, and I was so tired I couldn't move my legs. I felt like my heart was going to pop out of my chest, that I was going to have a stroke or a heart attack. I was done. I'd had it. I was just going to go home because this was crazy and way too much for anybody to handle. Some guys on the team had been through it for six years and survived. They told me that the previous year had been even harder.

During those hard times, my body had taken about all it could. I couldn't move. I couldn't touch the net, and I played horribly.

I was really discouraged; but then two thoughts came into my mind. First, I thought of my son, Ryder, and my wife, LaRee. I remembered that I was the provider for them and that they were counting on me every day and every moment. Second, I thought of Jesus and all the pain and suffering He went through. How people mocked Him and made fun of Him, but He held His head high and endured it all.

Those two thoughts kept me going. Every time I wanted to quit, I would think of those two pictures in my mind—my family and Jesus—and I kept going, taking it one minute at a time.

Eventually, my body adjusted and I became accustomed to those workouts and began to get my skills back. In fact, I started to play awesome.

Tau ended up making it to the finals of the Spanish League championships two years in a row and the Final Four of Europe both years I was there—a first for the franchise. We won the King's Cup, defeating Valencia for the championship.

The best playing tip I ever got was from my teammate Luis Scola at Tau. Luis later went on to play for the Houston Rockets. He said, "Play as hard as you can. Give everything you have in every practice and in every game, and it will all work out."

Taking Scola's advice, I played better and better and with more confidence. Before, I had tried to save myself for games. I didn't bring my all to practice. But that is the way Scola plays: full-out, all the time, every practice and every game.

In Spain, the coaches loved how hard I fought. I played like I cared. And I learned that to do anything well, you have to get it done in the trenches and earn it, because nothing is given to you.

Thoughts of quitting are usually mental wrestling matches. You can give in or you can overcome. Staying positive isn't easy, but a good attitude can work miracles.

Sometimes, you simply have to be a team player.

Many of us have a sense of entitlement. That is, many times we believe we are owed something. In basketball, many athletes believe they should play forty minutes a game. Some students in school believe they should always be given an A. When many kids turn sixteen, they believe they are entitled to be given a car to drive. Some potential missionaries believe their parents should pay for their missions and they don't have to work and save. Everything good in life comes from hard work and is a reward for earning what we get. It is tough and it takes sacrifice, but the harder you work, the more opportunities come your way and the happier you will be.

CHAPTER 10

The Secret of Life

There are many things that may happen to a person that bring changes to their life. For my family, important changes came out of a deep struggle, a real battle that tested our resolve. Through this cloud of discouragement, we found the secret of life.

The first time I saw LaRee was shortly after I returned from the Santiago Chile West Mission. It was September of 1999, when school was starting at Utah Valley State College. She walked by the Hall of Flags as my friends and I stood around waiting for class.

That picture is engraved inside my mind and will be forever. She had blonde hair, a beautiful summer tan, and wore a light brown skirt with sandals and a blue blouse. Seeing her made me feel like I had been punched in the face. "What was that? Wow, she's beautiful!"

Later that day I saw her again. A good friend of mine

asked her for her phone number as she walked by. I met her at a volleyball game and then again in the hall at school. She worked at a store in the University Mall, and I stopped to talk with her as I walked by with a group of friends. We hit it off, and I asked her on a date. After dating that fall and winter, I came to the conclusion that I just couldn't live without this girl.

We got engaged in April and were married in July 2000.

LaRee is so kind, so compassionate, and so much like my mom. I know that sounds silly, that you sometimes marry somebody like your mom, but that is exactly who she's like. LaRee is fun and creative, a great mother, very unselfish, and loves to help others. She has a strong testimony of Jesus Christ, is sensitive to the Spirit, and has great knowledge of the gospel. She is my best friend, which is more important than anything.

Our first son, Ryder, was born January 23, 2003, the first year I played for the Atlanta Hawks. These two special people quickly and easily became the centerpiece of my life.

Several years later, while I was traveling around Europe playing basketball, my wife was home hoping, praying, and crying over one of the most important challenges in our young marriage: secondary infertility.

In 2006 while in Victoria, Spain, LaRee found herself in the hospital with serious complications from a fertility treatment. We'd hoped and prayed for another child to join Ryder, but the costly procedure hadn't worked.

The hospital had no private rooms. One of the women

With our son Ryder on his first birthday.

sharing LaRee's room was screaming in pain. It was an ugly picture of agony and despair as she lay on that hospital bed on the other side of the world.

Shortly after LaRee was released from the hospital, I signed a contract to play for Dynamo in Moscow, Russia. When I left for Russia, LaRee traveled to California to see another specialist for another fertility treatment. In September 2006, she received an implantation and became pregnant. However, a few weeks later, just before she flew out to Russia with Ryder, she miscarried.

The winters in Russia are extremely cold and gloomy. Everything is overcast and gray. Even the snow has a dark, black shade to it. It didn't help LaRee's mood to be so far away from home with me traveling to practice and games.

All through that fall and the beginning of winter, she was sad and depressed.

We began to look into adoption, researching the possibilities in Russia and in the United States. Unfortunately, in Russia there is a lot of corruption and dishonesty in the adoption process. It's tough to know who to trust in a system that is broken.

One winter day, LaRee tuned in to the Oprah Winfrey Show where Oprah hosted a segment on orphans. The show highlighted the plight of orphans in the world who are sold for twenty dollars as child laborers. It showed orphans holding fishing nets in the sea. They were just thrown in the water to help with the nets, whether they could swim or not. Some of the children drowned; but the people in charge didn't care if a child died. They just went and bought another one.

Wheels started turning inside LaRee's head, and she had a strong feeling (that we believe was inspired) to research the problems of orphans in Russia. She felt there was a reason we had come to Russia, and it was more than just for basketball. That day on the sixteenth floor of a Russian apartment building, LaRee moved from being stuck, stalled, and stagnant to finding something she could believe in and do.

LaRee came across an analysis made by UNICEF about the predicament of orphans in Russia. There are approximately 600,000 orphans in Russia. Of those, 90 percent are social orphans, which means the government has deemed their parents unfit to raise them due to alcoholism, drugs, or other problems. The state simply takes the children away; but there are no foster homes in Russia. The children are taken to orphanages, dumped off, really, left to the fate of understaffed and underfunded facilities.

LaRee visited several orphanages around Moscow, and what she found was a living nightmare. They were all in very ill repair. While looking for orphanages she could help with, she came upon an orphanage in Lyubertsy, Russia. It was an old hospital with broken light fixtures, wires hanging from the ceilings, broken and filthy bathroom fixtures, and babies that didn't have enough caregivers around to hold them. They would just lie in their cribs all day, every day, having diaper changes whenever people could get to them. It was a system overloaded and overburdened from the fallout of a country's rampant problems and broken families.

The children were the victims.

"We have to do something, Travis," she told me.

We began working with some orphanages, but they just didn't feel right because of trust issues. When we met and got to know Tatyana Lilipova, director of the hospital in Lyubertsy, we decided to focus our work on that hospital. Tatyana is an amazing, loyal, and honest person we knew we could trust. Our work began there in January 2007.

It started out with just holding babies and giving them some attention and love. A few months later, it turned into physically upgrading the Lyubertsy hospital. We gathered what resources we could muster, involving other people in Russia and back in America. We were able to provide

With LaRee (left) and Tatyana Lilipova.

renovation of the electrical and plumbing systems and obtain furniture, cribs, tile, and television sets. Arrangements were made for staff and professional medical volunteers to provide health care, surgeries, and to just hold babies.

I made a phone call to the U.S. and asked my attorney David York to file papers to create a charitable foundation for us. The name we chose was the Little Heroes Foundation.

Soon, we forgot about our problems and filled our spare time with the work of bringing love to those who knew so little about it, the most vulnerable among us.

It changed our lives.

Ironically, but as if on cue, while LaRee was involved in the work with orphanages and after we had started the

Little Heroes
FOUNDATION

process to adopt a child in Moscow, LaRee called me one night after a game, screaming and yelling. My first thoughts were that something bad had happened, maybe Ryder was hurt.

"I'm pregnant!" she said.

"What? Are you serious?"

That's how we got our second son, Mason. After two failed in vitro fertilization procedures and several attempts to adopt, we were blessed with him naturally.

"Verily I say, men should be anxiously engaged in a good cause, and do many things of their own free will, and bring to pass much righteousness" (D&C 58:27).

Stop thinking about yourself all the time. My wife taught me a marvelous lesson that life is about more than just me. It is about helping others. In return, you help yourself. Don't wait for opportunities to come to you, seek them out. My wife got on her knees and specifically prayed, "Please give us opportunities to help others." Her faithful prayers were answered.

CHAPTER 11

Miracles Do Happen

S nap and pop.

It was one of Dynamo's biggest games of the 2007 season. We were playing against CSKA of Moscow, just months after the news about LaRee's pregnancy, and I was guarding former Duke University star Trajan Langdon when it happened.

Langdon had passed the ball into the post, and I went down to dig at center David Andersen as he kicked the ball back out to Langdon for a three-point shot. I made my move as Langdon took the shot but barely got an inch off the ground. It felt like Andersen had hit me in the back of the leg with a baseball bat. I immediately grabbed my calf, thinking I had pulled a muscle and contemplating the feeling that I was done, that my career was over. Teammates Lazaros Papadopoulos and Dmitri Domani dragged me over to the bench and then into the locker room.

I sat down and saw my foot just dangling there; I had no feeling in it. What I did have was a sick feeling in my stomach because I wasn't able to be there for my team and I was uncertain what had happened. A doctor examined my foot and told me I'd need major surgery—I had blown out my Achilles tendon.

I called LaRee because I knew she had been watching the game and would be concerned. I met with the coaches, manager, and trainer, and they told me they had doctors who could perform the operation. But I just wanted to go home, be with family, and find an American doctor in Utah to do the surgery.

The flight home was horrendous. I had to keep my foot elevated, and there was a risk of blood clots, which could be fatal. I called Rob Ramos, the head basketball trainer at BYU, and he arranged for a specialist, Dr. Robert Faux, to see me in Provo.

After a sixteen-hour flight from Moscow to Atlanta, we landed at around 8 P.M. I hadn't slept at all, and there was still the four-hour flight from Atlanta to Utah. The surgery was scheduled for 6 A.M. the morning after I arrived home.

But that all was the easy part. Wearing a cast and then a boot and undergoing rehab was the real challenge.

This injury couldn't have come at a busier time. I had just signed a big contract with Dynamo. I was playing for a legendary coach, Dušan Ivković, known as "Duda," who had coached all the big teams in Russia and Europe and won many championships. He was my friend, and he believed in me.

I was learning my best basketball from him, how to read defenses and how to slow down. We had a great team, making it to the top eight of the Euroleague. This injury came in one of the best seasons of my career.

Dynamo was wonderful to me during my recovery. They not only allowed me to fly home and have surgery with my own doctors but sent me videos of the games, paid me bonuses, and treated me like a member of their family.

I had also just become a Russian citizen.

Russian rules say you have to have two Russian players on the court at all times. It was a huge advantage for CSKA, our arch rival, to have J. R. Holden, who had gained his Russian citizenship, on their team. Before my injury, Duda and the owner of Dynamo came up with the idea to have me apply for Russian citizenship so Dynamo could have the same advantage.

The team put in the papers for me to become a Russian citizen and gain a Russian red passport. All the appropriate politicians and important citizens wrote letters to the government; but the application had to be signed by Russian president Vladimir Putin, a process that could take years.

When the day came, Putin had many tasks scheduled for his very busy day. He had to read and decide whether or not to sign papers for the likes of nuclear scientists and Nobel Prize candidates. There in the stack of papers was my

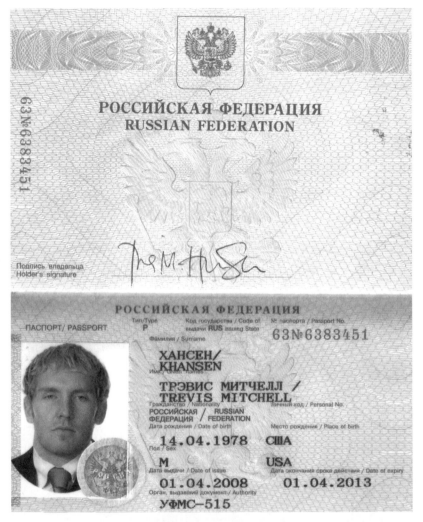

Official Russian passport.

application. He read through the information and signed it only a few months after we had applied.

One day the press showed up at practice in Moscow with TV cameras, and Dynamo's owners and general manager were there. It was to be announced that I had been approved for citizenship. It was amazing that this opportunity was offered to me and that it was actually granted.

The best news during that time, though, was that LaRee was expecting. We had always wanted a big family with a lot of kids. LaRee had prayed to Heavenly Father so hard to have more children, but the answer she was given was to not think about herself and start thinking about others. That's when, even though she couldn't speak any Russian, she began reaching out and offering help to the orphans in Russia.

I went to rehab twice a day and I had a cast on for two weeks. I was very blessed because the cast was originally supposed to be on for more like four to six weeks. I then graduated to a boot with an eight-inch heel that had discs inserted inside. Every two weeks, my medical team took a disc out to lower the heel and stretch it out. It was extremely painful.

Brett Mortensen is one of the greatest physical therapists around, and we became very close friends as he took care of me, pushed me, and brought me along the road to recovery. Only 10 percent of athletes come back from this kind of surgery. The night after the operation, I had a lot of friends and coaches come over to see me. It felt like a funeral. They were wishing me well, but in the backs of their minds, I knew they thought I was finished. So did I.

A standard procedure is to restructure the Achilles tendon so it is kind of loose; but Dr. Faux knew I was an athlete, and the decision was made to make it tight. He braided back the tendon like the mane of a horse. I had to put a book on my knee to straighten out the joint in therapy. I took blood thinners to decrease the chance of blood clots.

When the cast came off after two weeks, I almost fainted. I had never had surgery before. The scar was eight inches long and had staples in it. The first time the doctor grabbed my foot, I almost threw up.

I pushed myself in every way I could every day, and with the help of Mortensen I made it back to full health in six months. When I returned to Russia, Duda had retired and they had replaced him with Svetislav Pešić, a famous coach from Serbia whose team had defeated the United States. He came to Dynamo from Barcelona for a lot of money. After being hired, Pešić called me and said he wanted his doctors in Barcelona to examine me.

"I am in Utah spending time with family and would prefer not to travel to Barcelona during my summer vacation," I said.

The first day in the gym in Barcelona I was stretching out and Pešić came over to me. "I heard your agent said you are 100 percent."

"Yes, I am. It still swells up after I play, but I feel good," I said.

"Well," said Pešić. "You should fire your trainer and your doctors back home. Your face is fat and you look out of shape."

My next thoughts weren't the kindest I've ever had.

We have all had someone call us names, talk behind our backs, judge us, or treat us unfairly. We have all had sorrows, heartaches, worries, sadness, and pain. If we can get past blaming others, we can learn to soar. Take your life into your own hands and what happens? A special thing, there is no one to blame.

Where does the power lie? In you.

Pešić wanted me to run ten miles in the mountains. Mountain runs are a big deal in Europe.

"I can't do that yet," I replied. To do that just coming back from surgery didn't seem wise to me.

"Your agent said you are 100 percent, and if you can't run this distance, then we have a problem."

I came up close to him with an intense look in my eyes and answered, "If you play me, I will help you win games. Your job is to win and I know how to help you do that."

I thought to myself, "Just give me a chance to play. I know I can help."

In my first game back, I scored twenty-six points against Serbia and we won the initial tournament of the preseason. But I wasn't the same. I didn't have the same snap in my jump, and I was a little slower. I couldn't play defense like I once could, but I was happy to be back on the floor where I belonged.

That 2007 season, I ended up having the best year of my career, averaging 19 points a game. I shot 63 percent from the field, 53 percent from beyond the three-point line, and 90 percent from the free-throw line.

Before I returned to Russia for this big comeback, one day after a rehabilitation workout, I took my crutches and walked

Renovation work at Lyubertsy hospital in Russia.

into the Bajio Mexican Grill in Provo. When I sat down to eat lunch, Eric Graves, the international marketing director for Nature's Sunshine, came over and introduced himself to me.

"Are you Travis Hansen?" he asked.

"Yes," I replied, having just sat down with my wife.

"I read that *Deseret News* article by Dick Harmon about you in Russia and the work you're doing with your charity."

"Oh, yeah. We have done some fun things. It's just getting started," I said.

"Well, Travis, we do a lot of business in Russia. Maybe our company could get involved and help," he said.

"We'd love it," I answered.

It wasn't just idle talk. He came through.

In the ensuing months, the IRS accepted our papers to establish Little Heroes as a 501(c)(3) charity. When we

Finished work on a room in Lyubertsy. New floor, cots, and storage.

returned to Russia, with help from Nature's Sunshine, and others, we began making serious changes in the Lyubertsy hospital.

In Moscow, word got out about this work, and one of the biggest sports magazines in Russia printed a story on me entitled "Missionary." It looked not only at my basketball career but at my Mormon mission experience in Chile and the charitable work LaRee and I had done in Russia. When the work on the Lyubertsy hospital was finally finished, the press wanted to have a tour. While taking reporters and photographers around the orphanage that day, I just happened to hear a mother crying in one of the rooms. I went in to see why.

What transpired in the next few moments led to one of the greatest miracles I have ever seen.

CHAPTER 12

Artem

When you are down by two points or the game is tied and only a few ticks remain on the clock, you hope for a buzzer beater. It's a shot that wins the game. But the basketball court isn't the only place where people hope and pray for a buzzer beater. Several years ago in Moscow, two-year-old Artem's family was also searching for a way to beat the clock.

Their desires were intense because Artem's life didn't involve basketball or game-winning three-point shots, but hospital stays, doctors, and a failing liver.

A week before my press tour that day at Lyubertsy hospital, I had received a call from Dr. Igor Cojocaru of Moscow. He had read the "Missionary" article and told me he would like to get involved in some way. I thanked him and kept his number handy. His and many other names were in the back of my mind, coupled with thoughts of gratitude for their offers of help, as I led the press through the halls at Lyubertsy.

When I heard the tormented cry from a mother in one of the hospital rooms, I motioned for the tour to stop briefly and went into the room. As I walked through the doorway, I saw a woman wailing in agony as she hovered over her two-year-old child. His name was Artem, and he was all gray and green with jaundice. The director of the hospital told me his liver had failed and he needed a transplant or he would die within a few weeks. In Russia, it was typical to let someone in this situation just pass—there was little they could do.

"Let's do something," I told the director on the spot. "We have to do something."

And so I called Dr. Cojocaru and told him about Artem.

"That is my specialty," he said. "I am a transplant specialist."

In fact, Dr. Cojocaru was an expert in the field and had recently been offered a job in St. Louis, Missouri, to do liver transplants.

It was as if the seconds ticking off on the clock had just stopped, giving us hope that there might be a way for Artem to pull through.

Dr. Cojocaru immediately drove out to Lyubertsy to examine Artem. Once there, he quickly put Artem on a feeding tube and told the other doctors to back away and let him take over. (That's kind of how you get things done in Russia.) He made a plan to give Artem a healthy foundation

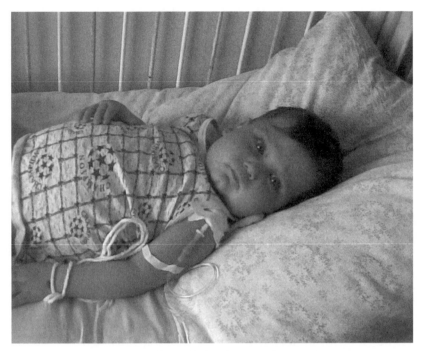

Artem in Lyubertsy before his miracle transplant.

in preparation for surgery and a transplant. And then the search for a donor and a transplant team began.

Dr. Cojocaru and I wrote letters to the top hospitals in the United States and Europe, asking for a free transplant. No one could do it. Artem's stepfather said he would be a donor. But Russian law mandated that transplants are illegal unless they come from a blood relative.

Still, we continued to look for a location and hope for a miracle. Finally, a medical center in Belgium said they could do a transplant there for $100,000. We'd need to get that funding, but it brought us a little closer to our goal.

Then, one night after a game, I got word that a liver

was available. We'd have to ignore the law about transplants coming from blood relatives, but that could work. We just needed the money. I called LaRee, whose first thought was about Jesus' parable of the rich man who chose to lay up his riches on earth instead of heaven (see Luke 12:13–21).

"Let's pay for it," LaRee said. "Let's save this little boy."

That very night Artem received his new liver. Today he is a happy, healthy child who is on his way to more of a life than anyone gave him a chance for that winter day in 2007 when I happened to hear his mother's cries.

Dr. Cojocaru waived his fees for Artem's surgery, and from that night forward, he got anesthesiologists to likewise donate their fees and organized volunteer doctors from Belgium, Germany, and other parts of Europe to be on call to help in future surgeries. In the months and years to follow, his team of volunteers has helped many children throughout Europe to obtain life-saving surgeries.

This is the reason LaRee and I were prompted to help and why we feel we were sent to Russia. The Lord wanted us to get this done and He allowed us to play a part in all of this. We were instruments in His hands.

In a letter LaRee wrote to her brother Cody on his mission, she said:

> I am so thankful for trials and humility and especially the Atonement. . . .
> I remember when I learned I would not be able to have children again without in vitro or a miracle.

Artem up and happy after his miracle transplant.

I was so alone and heartbroken. [It made] me so humble, I was open to anything the Lord wanted me to do. I prayed, saying, "I've done everything possible," and simply turned it all over to him. That is all I had to do. It was no longer in my hands. I pleaded with him to guide me and do his will.

My heart was completely open and broken. That is when the Spirit guided me to open the Little Heroes Foundation. I know my mission was to help children in Russia. I knew that I was there for some purpose, and my fertility problems were to guide and humble me. I am so thankful for the Atonement. I was never alone. He knew how I was feeling and was there for me. I then realized my problems were small.

I needed to stop feeling sorry for myself and think of others. Think of all the children in Russia who could use some help.

President Ezra Taft Benson said, "The Lord works from the inside out. The world works from the outside in. The world would take people out of the slums. Christ takes the slums out of people, and then they take themselves out of the slums. The world would mold men by changing their environment. Christ changes men, who then change their environment. [The world] would shape human behavior, but Christ can change human nature."[1]

Since the Little Heroes Foundation was formed in 2007, with the help of many generous people, especially our founding sponsor Nature's Sunshine, the work has expanded to many areas outside of Moscow and Lyubertsy hospital.

By the end of 2012 it is estimated more than 210,000 lives will have been improved because of the efforts of the Little Heroes Foundation created by LaRee Hansen. The work has impacted people in Mali, West Africa; Santiago, Chile; and Birendranagar, Nepal.

Since its beginning, the charity has renovated a children's hospital in Russia, has built two schools in Africa, and has built a health clinic in Nepal. The Foundation has improved the development of 154 handicapped children, found safe homes for 298 foster children, provided 395 life-sustaining

In Mali, where the first Little Heroes Academy
was built in the village of Mana.

surgeries, and provided 2,377 Christmas gifts to children and families in stress. The Little Heroes Foundation has brought about educational opportunities for 2,680 children, improved the living conditions of 3,744 people while helping 5,784 overcome disease and addictions, directed medical treatments for 62,297, and served 338,950 nutritious meals to children who would have otherwise gone hungry.

A miracle is an extraordinary event manifesting divine intervention in human affairs. Artem and the Little Heroes Foundation were our drops in the bucket and are just one of the many reasons we were led to Russia.

CHAPTER 13

Comebacks, Decisions, Directions

I t was a game I will never forget.

It was also an afternoon I learned a lot about seizing the opportunity to change your momentum if you find yourself going in the wrong direction.

It was the BYU-Utah rivalry game in the Marriott Center February 23, 2002; and for twenty-two minutes the Utes had been beating us down. I was in foul trouble, and everything looked bleak. We were behind twenty-one points and had little business even thinking we could win this game.

The Marriott Center was packed, the game was on TV regionally, and we were trying to help Steve Cleveland get BYU's program back to where it belonged as regular conference champions. The entire first half we were completely dominated by Utah, a team featuring Britton and Jeff Johnsen, Travis Spivey, and Nick Jacobson.

We left the floor at halftime for the locker room and

were disappointed to say the least. The mood was somber and silent. I was mad at myself. It wasn't supposed to be easy, but this? Getting killed at home? No way.

Something had to change.

We had a ritual before games where everyone would gather around me and I'd yell out things like, "Are we going to win?" The guys would reply, "Sei-sensay." And then we'd do our best karate-chop motions and run out on the court hyped up. I was contemplating making the team do some sort of similar, amped-up mid-game ritual, anything we could to go crazy and get things going. It was that bad.

We sat in the locker room with our heads hung low, Jared Jensen, our center; Mark Bigelow; and seniors Matt Montague, Eric Nielsen, and I. In came assistant coach Dave Rose and director of operations Brian Santiago. They said just a few sentences: "You are faster, you are stronger, you can play with these guys. We know you can win this game. We believe in you. We are not a .500 team, we are a play-off team and an NCAA tournament team. We believe in you."

The speech gave us an extraordinary boost in confidence. In that moment, they didn't berate us. Instead, they made us believe we were better than we were. It was really amazing. Our confidence soared.

We came out of the locker room for the second half and outscored Utah 37 to 18. Montague had 7 assists and tied Danny Ainge's career record for assists (539) in that game. We won 63–61 in one of the biggest comebacks in school history.

Official BYU jersey.

With 1:18 left in the game, Montague hit a three-pointer to bring BYU within one, 61–60. . . . Then Montague made a record-setting assist to Nielsen who finished the play by hitting an eight-foot jumper to give the Cougars their first lead of the game, 62–61, with 25 seconds remaining. . . .

A crucial rebound and one made free throw by BYU upstart Dan Howard gave the Cougars a two-point edge, 63–61, and then Mark Bigelow sealed the victory with a rebound off a Utah jump shot. Bigelow finished with 11 points and two rebounds. . . .

Despite being in foul trouble, Cougar Travis Hansen led the comeback as he has done so many times during the season. He finished with a game-high 17 points in addition to his seven rebounds and three assists.[1]

The 43 points we gave up to Utah in the first half were the most we'd surrendered all year. The eighteen we allowed them in the second half tied the lowest we'd allowed any team all season.

What changed from the first to second half? It was our attitude, direction, and momentum.

One of the toughest things to do in life is to always be at the top of your game. We've been asked to give all our hearts to so many things, to be committed and perform, that sometimes it's impossible not to get down, distracted, or simply run out of energy.

We read in the scriptures, "Serve him with all your heart and with all your soul" (Joshua 22:5) and "love the Lord your God with all your heart and with all your soul" (Deuteronomy 13:3).

But what happens in those times when all your heart isn't totally with it? What do you do?

A simple answer might be: Obey and pray. Do what you know is right and correct. Pray for the energy, direction, and momentum to carry you where you want to go. And pray for the willingness to make a change in direction when it becomes clear you are not on a winning path.

One of the worst moments I had in sports came my senior year at BYU when we played Kansas State during the Paradise Jam tournament in the Virgin Islands.

I was a very passionate player. At times, I had an anger management issue. During this particular game, that passion and anger combined to create a moment of which I'm not very proud. The officials were making calls I didn't agree with. I felt that my teammates weren't pulling their weight. I wanted to win! At one point I watched a teammate knock down a member of the opposing team. My teammate apologized and helped the guy up. I was appalled. I wanted to get after these guys, beat them, get them down and kick them! Obviously, I was pretty frustrated.

And then, on the way down the court late in this game, I was called for a foul and I just lost it. I went over to the padded area around the upright support that held the backboard and hit it. I was immediately called for my second technical foul and kicked out of the game.

We were down by only two points in the fourth quarter and I'd just been kicked out of the game. I'd wanted to win so badly that I'd lost my temper. But it didn't end there. I went into the locker room and I was fuming. I selfishly started blaming my teammates for not showing enough passion in the game. To demonstrate my own superior passion, I began destroying the locker room. It's a moment I am not proud of, and it was wrong.

We ended up winning that game, then the next, and ultimately won the tournament. When we returned to Provo we were called in for a film session. Coach Rose came in just before the video started.

"We have one problem on this team," said Rose. And he pointed directly at me.

That was the last thing I thought would happen. I was shocked, then embarrassed. I couldn't believe it. But then, something inside me told me he was right.

Of course, Coach Rose was right. I was the problem.

"You don't know how others react when you lose your cool. You don't realize what it does to your teammates and your coaches, how it affects the game when you are out of control and don't show leadership," Coach Rose yelled at me before walking out the door.

We didn't watch videos that day, instead we just went out on the floor and had practice. It was a very low point for me in my career and in my life. It hurt, but he was right, and I needed to hear that.

On that day, in that moment, I determined I would change. I was totally wrong, and I knew it. I don't think I got another technical foul after that game. Coach Rose changed my outlook, how I focused my energy, and how I played. From then on, I tried to keep myself in control and have a better attitude about my teammates.

There was another time my heart was in the right place but my actions did not prove it, and I had to make a correction.

I had just returned from my mission to Chile. I dearly missed my mother and was struggling with the whys of her death. Some of my friends were getting tattoos. In the basketball world, tattoos are a big thing. Having one would help me fit in. Plus, I was intrigued with getting something that would remind me of my mother.

And so, without much thought, I went to a shop and, for about a hundred bucks, walked back out with "The Heavens" tattooed on my shoulder. I didn't think anyone would really care, and I didn't show it to anybody.

A few months later, in October 2000, President Gordon B. Hinckley spoke in priesthood conference and counseled against marking up our bodies with tattoos: "Now comes the craze of tattooing one's body. I cannot understand why any young man—or young woman, for that matter—would wish to undergo the painful process of disfiguring the skin with various multicolored representations of people, animals, and various symbols. With tattoos, the process is permanent, unless there is another painful and costly undertaking to remove it. Fathers, caution your sons against having their bodies tattooed. They may resist your talk now, but the time will come when they will thank you. A tattoo is graffiti on the temple of the body."[2]

That had an impact on me. A prophet of the Lord condemning tattoos! I immediately wanted to get it off. Here I was, playing at BYU, an athlete who should probably be setting an example for his team and our fans. I started thinking about what I would tell my children one day if they asked why I hadn't followed the prophet. I thought of what the tattoo would look like when I was old. (Not pretty!)

It turns out that having a tattoo was the opposite of what I thought it would be. It didn't make me cool or feel accepted by others. I wanted it removed. I saw a doctor and began laser treatments to have the tattoo removed. For five minutes, a laser would burn my skin to start the removal process. But the real pain came in the five hours following each treatment. It felt like my skin was cooking, like it was burning. After three treatments, it was gone.

My entire mentality changed when I heard the prophet speak. It changed my direction and my attitude. Today, I'll tell anyone who is thinking of having a tattoo not to do it. Getting a tattoo hurts; but it hurts even more to take it off and it costs ten times as much to erase what you shouldn't have done in the first place.

Changing directions takes some courage. It means admitting you've made a mistake and being willing to make a course correction. Heavenly Father loves each of us. I'm certain it was His Spirit, through the gift of the Holy Ghost, that really touched me when I heard the words of the prophet and received some well-deserved chastisement from my coach. Listen to the voices of reason. When they cheer you on, warn you away, or simply suggest backing off, make the change. You'll be happy you did.

CHAPTER 14

Me, Me, Me versus We

Luis Scola is one of the best basketball players in the world. At six foot nine, this native of Argentina is extremely agile, with long arms and a soft touch around the basket. He looks a little like actor Antonio Banderas, or at least he wishes he does.

Before he came to the NBA and established himself as a star for the Houston Rockets, Scola played with me in Europe. His kindness and friendship is something that taught me a great lesson.

When I left the Atlanta Hawks to play for Tau in Spain, it was kind of scary. I felt like I wasn't totally in control of things. I didn't know my future coaches, trainers, or teammates. I had no idea what my living arrangements would be like. When I walked out of our town house in Provo and headed to the airport for my flight to Spain, I began to cry. I would be traveling far away from my family and all I could

With teammate and friend Luis Scola.

think about was how much I'd miss them. Everything would be new and unknown to me.

When I got to Spain, I didn't know where I was. I didn't have an alarm clock in my hotel room. I didn't even know what time it was. I stayed up most of the first night wondering how I'd make it on time and be prepared for my first day with the team. It was horrible.

That morning I had my physical examination and walked into the gym to get ready for practice. Luis came over to me. He was the best basketball player on my team and probably in all of Europe, and I felt out of place.

"Hey, Travis, I'm so happy to have you on this team. We have heard all about you. If there is anything I can do for you, please tell me and I'll do it."

He made me feel welcome and wanted and needed. His kindness didn't end on the gym floor but was part of film sessions and events away from basketball. He invited me to his house for an Argentine barbecue. When my son Ryder had a birthday, Luis came over with a present, and it made Ryder's day.

Scola made a great impression on me. He was the nicest, most amazing human being. He wasn't a Christian; I don't think he even believed in God. But he was a friend who taught me a great lesson: just be nice to people. It can make such a huge difference. I thought back to my high school days. How big a difference could it have made to others if I would have walked up to them in the cafeteria or in class and introduced myself? If I had just asked how they were doing and made them feel more comfortable? It's such a small thing, but it can go a long way.

I didn't have much control over anything when I left for Spain, but I had to make the most of it, and Scola's friendship was a huge help—an answer to prayer at a time when I couldn't change my circumstances but trusted the Lord to send someone or something to make them easier.

In life, we can't always control what happens to us. What we can control is how we react when life throws a curveball. The first step is pray always (see 2 Nephi 32:9; 3 Nephi 18:15; D&C 90:24). Pray for strength, pray for courage, pray for understanding, pray for comfort. If your desire is righteous and if you ask in all humility, your prayers will be

Scan this QR code (or visit http://youtu.be/5QOkK e55-2o) to hear Travis talk about the power of kindness.

answered. You will receive promptings of what to do. When you act on *those* promptings, you will receive *more* promptings. That's how the process works.

It's happened for me many times. And it is exactly what led to the adoption of our third child.

For most of our married lives, LaRee and I have prayerfully sought for the blessing of having more children. Several years after our son Ryder was born, we again wanted to have a child. When it became clear that it wouldn't be easy to conceive, we sought fertility treatments and medical procedures, we prayed a lot, we discussed adoption, and ultimately we received an answer to set aside our pursuits and focus on serving others for a time. Shortly thereafter, we started the Little Heroes Foundation, and then LaRee became pregnant again—a true miracle—and our son Mason was born. Seeking another child a few years later, we again began praying and looking into adoption.

As we researched options, it became clear to us how wonderful adoption is. One of the things that stood out to me was the opportunity we would be giving a child to change the outcome of his or her life by providing a future much different from the one he or she was born into. I came across a list of remarkable individuals who had been adopted. The list included Olympic figure skater Scott Hamilton; Dave Thomas, the founder of the Wendy's restaurant chain; country singer Faith Hill; Baseball Hall of Fame announcer Harry Cary; actor Jamie Foxx; NFL quarterback Dante Culpepper; NBA center Alonzo Mourning; poet and author,

Maya Angelou; First Lady Eleanor Roosevelt; and the late Steve Jobs, co-founder of Apple Computers and the man who gave us the iPod.[1]

Learning about the adoption process and the positive impact it could have on so many lives inspired us. LaRee and I knew it was the right decision, and our answers came in a lightning-quick fashion.

As has become typical in our lives, good things tend to happen when I go down. Our adoption miracle occurred right after I was seriously injured on the basketball court. It was near the end of April 2010, and I was practicing with Real in Madrid, Spain, preparing for the play-offs. I came off a pick set by seven-foot center Darius Lavrinovič and hit another player, which knocked me flat on my back. I had no feeling in my legs.

It was scary for a few moments. The feeling in my legs didn't return for about ten seconds, and the gym fell silent. People tried to help me up off the floor but I couldn't get up on my own power. After diagnostic tests, doctors determined I had broken my fourth and fifth lumbar vertebrae. The ligament protruded out and pressed on my sciatic nerve.

I tried therapy, but after a few days the pain and numbness down my leg wasn't getting any better. We made preparations to return to the United States for back surgery.

I was devastated to have back surgery at such a young age. My back muscles were shredded, and I had to start from scratch. After surgery they had to teach me how to sit up. Rolling to my side felt like I had a thirty-pound sandbag around my waist. We prayed for help and found encouragement in the knowledge that at least we were near friends and family and my favorite physical therapist during this challenge.

What we didn't know at first was that being in Utah would prove very fortuitous in the next few days. If not for the injury, we would not have been in Utah or even in the United States at the time. LaRee had been intensely interested in adoption since we left Spain. She had a friend who had given her a password to log on to an adoption agency called A Guardian Angel Adoptions in West Jordan, Utah. She got online and studied the possibilities when she could, but things were busy around the time of my surgery, and LaRee hadn't had time to check the website for a while.

One day, she went back to the website and saw something that really touched her heart. She rushed over to where I was lying on the couch and said, "Travis, listen to this."

A young girl was having a baby girl in June. She was traveling to Utah that very week to get situated with the doctors, the agency, and living conditions. As LaRee read the information, we both looked at each other and felt that this girl was different, this girl was special. LaRee immediately called the agency and asked if there was any way she could place a profile folder in the hands of this expectant mother.

"You know," said the agency worker, "there are a lot of people who want to adopt but, yes, we will allow you to put together a profile. However, we need it in a couple of days.

This woman is flying into Utah in a few days to get adapted and prepare for delivery the first week of June."

On May 20, the young woman got off the plane in Salt Lake City and went into labor early. The agency called and said if we wanted to be considered, we'd have to get our profile to West Jordan that night. We met the agency representative at a gas station in West Jordan and delivered the folder containing our family information, a profile of our employment and background information, and photographs of our family.

We drove back to our home in Orem and waited, hoping to hear something soon. Twenty-four hours later the phone rang. When I saw it was the agency calling, I put it on speaker mode. The voice at the other end said, "Would you like to come up and see your baby?"

Tears filled LaRee's eyes and ran down her cheeks. We got a babysitter and left for the hospital.

Adoption is a very special thing. It is very spiritual, wonderful, and scary all at the same time.

We went in a room and sat with the social worker. We were asked to sign adoption papers before we saw the baby or the mother. Then they brought in this beautiful baby girl and we were able to hold Halle for a few hours before they took her back to her mother.

This young mother was beautiful, very nice, and so kind, but her situation was not one in which she could raise this baby. She was so unselfish to give up her child, her flesh and blood, and hand this baby over to someone else. Can you

With newborn Halle.

imagine how that would feel? Can you imagine how much faith and hope she must have needed to place that little life in the arms of strangers and know all would be well? Can you imagine the trust she had in us and how much responsibility that then became for us?

Halle became a part of our family May 21, 2010, one day after her birth on May 20. LaRee had looked on that website May 16. We'd been in Utah less than a month when things began to fall into place. After the required six-month waiting period, the adoption was legally complete. On December 23, 2010, we took our most wonderful Christmas gift, Halle, to the Mount Timpanogos Utah Temple, where she was sealed to us. It was one of the most amazing, spiritual, and unforgettable experiences I've ever had in my life.

LaRee with Halle on December 23, 2010.

Adoption teaches us that we don't always get to choose our path or situation, but we can choose to make the best of it. We can wake up in the morning and choose to be positive or negative; to do what is right or wrong.

LaRee and I were not given what we always wanted, six or eight children of our own; but we have been blessed with two precious boys and the opportunity to adopt a beautiful little girl. It is amazing that she is ours, our own little girl. Her birth mother wrote us a letter and told us she felt that Halle was always meant to be ours; we feel the same.

Halle will look back someday and see many different endings or paths her life may have taken. Hopefully, the life she has with us will be one of love, structure, support,

Adoption day! Halle legally became ours in December 2010.

kindness, and mutual respect, and we can give her the best chance possible to grow, mature, and succeed in all she dreams to do and be.

LaRee was inspired to look on that website. She sought this blessing of adoption. She begged for the opportunity, and her prayers were answered. Sometimes God has blessings for us, but He waits for us to ask for them before He sends them into our lives.

It was like it was meant to be. If I hadn't hurt my back, we would have been in the European play-offs, half a world away, and Halle would not have come into our family. I had surgery May 2 and Halle came home to us May 22.

Halle is so sweet, beautiful, funny, and dramatic. She is a princess and loves pretending she is a mom. She's always

Halle.

cuddling her dolls, rocking them, and talking to them. She is, in every way, a little girl.

After having had two sons, it is amazing to see the bond that grows between a father and daughter. It is amazing how they look to you, see you as their father—their protector—and how you feel that responsibility come upon you. It is a natural bond.

It's great to see her fold her arms during family home evening and try to be and act like her brothers. Ryder sits on one side, Mason on the other, and they all just adore each other. They have no blood relation but they know they love each other. They know they are brother and sister. It's amazing and humbling to see.

In reality, we are all brothers and sisters and come from the same Heavenly Father. We need to be on the same team.

We need to look out for each other, be kind to one another, dish out assists, magnify the team over the glorification of the one.

Jesus said, "This is my commandment, That ye love one another, as I have loved you. Greater love hath no man than this, that a man lay down his life for his friends" (John 15:12–13).

CHAPTER 15

The Hero within You

Playing under bright lights in front of noisy crowds, dunking the basketball, chasing down loose balls, defending world-class athletes, knocking down threes, and getting paid in the process is a dream only a few can comprehend. It was a thrill.

However, LaRee and I had predetermined that when our oldest son, Ryder, turned eight, I'd retire from playing basketball and settle down to a normal role as father and husband. This was our goal all along, and my career ended the fall of 2011. My last competitive game as a pro came as a member of Khimki in Moscow, Russia.

What did I learn from all these experiences? From Little League to Mountain View High School in Orem, from Utah Valley State College to BYU, from the Atlanta Hawks to my career in the European basketball leagues in Spain and Russia—what did it all teach me?

With Ryder on his baptism day.

One answer I could give is I learned how to work hard.

Playing sports taught me to set goals, how to reach goals, and—when I failed—how to deal with failing. I learned how to develop a strong mentality—a winner's mentality—and how to deal with others. I learned to push myself and reach my potential. Basketball taught me I could push harder than I ever imagined. I reached levels of mental and physical performance I never thought I could, and much of that is due to the diligent work and faith of my coaches and trainers who expected a lot of me and believed in me.

In Europe, I played with many outstanding athletes who

later found themselves on NBA rosters. These include Jose Calderon (Toronto Raptors), Luis Scola (Houston Rockets), Andres Nocioni (Philadelphia 76ers), and Tiago Splitter (San Antonio Spurs).

Playing with these great athletes was the experience of a lifetime. But there is another answer I could give if asked what I learned from all my years of playing basketball.

I could say that I learned that basketball doesn't really matter. That being in the NBA, being amongst the best, most talented players in the world doesn't really matter. The most important thing that should matter to everyone is that you believe in Jesus Christ and follow Him. In the Sacred Grove, God said, "This is My Beloved Son. Hear Him" (Joseph Smith—History 1:17).

Success in life isn't based on if you played in the NBA or the NFL or if you're the richest guy on the block or the smartest guy in class. It doesn't matter. I totally believe that. Jesus taught, "a man's life consisteth not in the abundance of the things which he possesseth" (Luke 12:15). What really matters is what you do with what you have been given.

In my life, I've been called many things. Many of my friends and fans have put labels on me, calling me nick-names they thought defined me. In high school I was known as Poppy and AG for "Always Grounded," because I was always getting punished and grounded.

At BYU and in the NBA my nicknames were Eminem and Elder 8 Mile because I looked like the white rap singer from Detroit. In Spain, fans called me *El Mormón,* and in

Russia, they called me Mormon Sniper after I became a great three-point shooter.

As a retired professional athlete, I've learned that all those nicknames do not matter; it's what I do that counts. I'd trade it all to be called trusted, dependable, faithful, loyal, and a true disciple of Jesus Christ. Those are the nicknames that really matter.

My wife, LaRee, is a remarkable companion and friend. The work she has done in answer to her most fervent prayers has set a high course for our family and our future. These are LaRee's words and counsel to our children and me. I find this advice of absolute importance for anyone striving to find peace and direction in their lives:

When times get hard and discouraging, never, ever give up.

Pray to Heavenly Father and ask to feel our Savior's love and comfort. He knows you and has felt how you are feeling. You are never alone. He is a prayer away.

You are powerful beyond measure. Dreams are blueprints of our future. We need to dream to succeed. Never, ever stop dreaming and believing.

Pray for strength every day that you can make your dreams come true and help others achieve theirs.

Love yourself. You are a child of God, a prince and a princess of a righteous King. You are royalty.

Be confident. Confidence is a priceless possession. You are a one and only. Be proud of who you are.

Don't be afraid of failing. Keep trying!

Be compassionate and giving. Be an instrument in the Lord's hands. Help others along the way, and give more than you take. Try to put yourself in the shoes of others.

Don't judge or gossip. Meet everyone with an open heart and mind. Try to find good in everyone. Love. Love with all your heart, mind, and strength. Love the gospel, love life, love your neighbors and all mankind. We are all spirit brothers and sisters, children of our Father in Heaven.

Forgive and forget. Don't hold grudges, you will only hurt yourself. Let go of what has hurt you and move on. That is the only way you will feel peace with yourself and others around you.

Learn from your mistakes. It is never too late to change. Use the Atonement and gain a testimony of it. You can get peace back into your life. Every day try to be a better person. Strive to keep the commandments and strengthen your testimony. A testimony is priceless. You need one! It is a lifesaver. Please gain one.

Read the scriptures and use them to help with problems and questions. Study them; knowledge of them is eternal.

Look at the beautiful creations around you. Enjoy

nature and the sunsets. Take a minute to reflect on God's creations. Notice rainbows, flowers, and trees. There is so much beauty all around; never get too busy to notice the small things, like a baby smiling your way. Smile back and look into those innocent eyes.

Always, always remember we can be together forever someday. I love you, and I am always with you. I am your mother, your wife, and I am your friend. I am so very proud of you.

Those are powerful words from a faithful woman who has been by my side from Provo to Moscow and points in between.

Basketball? It's fun and games. Life's challenges? Now, those are real. I think LaRee provides an accurate road map to follow.

We inevitably will face challenges in completing goals and dreams. Anyone who has started a diet or an exercise program can attest to the commitment level that exists in the beginning. You start off full of energy, bound and determined to lose weight, get buff, whatever. But then one day, you're tired, or a good show is on TV, or you just don't feel like it, or maybe there's an open bag of Doritos sitting there calling your name. Whatever the goal, every worthy objective will have its accompanying challenges—it's then that we find out how truly committed we are.

President Gordon B. Hinckley said:

There are forces all around us that would deter us from that effort. The world is constantly crowding in on us. From all sides we feel the pressure to soften our stance, to give in here a little and there a little.

We must never lose sight of our objective. We must ever keep before us the goal which the Lord has set for us [and the goals we have set for ourselves]. . . .

We must stand firm. We must hold back the world. If we do so, the Almighty will be our strength and our protector, our guide and our revelator. We shall have the comfort of knowing that we are doing what He would have us do. Others may not agree with us, but I am confident that they will respect us. We will not be left alone. . . .

I believe that others will rally around us if we will do so. We can stand for truth and goodness, and we will not stand alone. Moreover, we shall have the unseen forces of heaven to assist us.[1]

During the next few years, the decisions and actions you make and take, will change your life and define what direction your future will take. You can set your compass the right direction right now. You can realize your dreams by setting goals and having a plan. You can find happiness by remembering whose royal blood flows through your veins; it comes from your Heavenly Father, who is not limited and has not put a cap on your potential.

I am convinced, beyond a doubt, there is a hero that lies within every one of us, a person that can make a difference in this world every day in countless ways. Many of us hide that power. We need to find it.

The dictionary defines "hero" in the following ways: "A mythological or legendary figure often of divine descent endowed with great strength or ability; an illustrious warrior; a man admired for his achievements and noble qualities; one that shows great courage; the principal male character in a literary or dramatic work, or the central figure in an event, period or movement."[2]

All these definitions describe roles you can take on in these latter-day times and seasons. I encourage you to find the hero that is within you. You can make a difference to yourself and others if you believe in yourself and your cause and try with everything you have been given.

A ball can't go in the hoop without a shooter. You can never win without entering the game.

Is it in you?

Yes. It is in us all.

THE NEXT
FEW YEARS
WILL
CHANGE
YOUR LIFE

WORKBOOK

Create a Plan,
Set Goals, and
Find the Hero Within

I would like to discuss with you about how the next few years will change your life. You are at an important and crucial time in your life. If you have not done it already, then today is the day to use the following four steps to find success and true peace and happiness.

In Alma 37, we learn the four steps to ensuring you will always be successful, truly happy, and at peace.

Let me share with you the formula and its four important points. In verses 6–7 Alma teaches his son that by "small and simple things are great things brought to pass." To some of you what I am about to explain may seem insignificant, but I promise you that if you will reflect upon your

Scan this QR code (or visit http://youtu.be/O6t-ayN 7xg4) to hear Travis teach this formula.

life you will realize that this small and simple formula has kept you safe and blessed your life as you have followed it, maybe even without knowing that this is the formula!

First, pray. Prayer is the primary communication between you and your Father in Heaven. Prayer opens the doors to heaven and has the capability to change the night to day (see Alma 37:36–37).

Second, read the scriptures. You need to study the scriptures, especially the Book of Mormon; it is counsel from our Heavenly Father, our Savior, and prophets of God. As you read it you will be given answers to your prayers, and promptings will come to you (see Alma 37:1–9).

Third, be obedient. You need to be obedient by keeping the commandments so that you can be safe, protected, and feel the influence and guidance of the Holy Ghost (see Alma 37:35).

Fourth, give service. This is your responsibility and one of the greatest joys in life. One of our greatest mistakes as humans is when we walk through life with our eyes closed and lose out on those opportunities to serve (see Alma 37:34).

This formula is what has enabled me, my family, and many people we look up to and follow to enjoy a beautiful, happy life. These steps are essential to have as the foundation in your life before you start dreaming, creating a plan, setting goals, and striving to find the hero within.

Create a Plan

Identifying Your Dreams

"The key to happiness is having dreams. The key to success is making your dreams come true."

—Author unknown

The first step in creating your plan is to create a dream board. You need to find or draw pictures that represent what you want in life. Maybe it's a house, car, degree, attending a specific university, a career, or even getting married in your favorite temple. Draw or find images that represent these things and paste them here or in your journal. As you do this activity, be excited and specific, and be willing to believe that anything is possible.

What are your big dreams?

What do you see yourself doing five, ten, or fifteen years from now?

Your dreams are essentially what you want. And as you think and ponder what you want, your dreams will

MY DREAM BOARD

constantly be on your mind. And that will give you a vision and direction and help you get to where you want to go. Dreams are imaginings of what we can make happen in our life.

A seed grows in the soil before it appears shooting through to the sunlight. But with dreams come great responsibility. It is just not enough to dream and forget about that dream.

Many people dream, but only some wake up and work for it. It is essential to work hard for your dreams. Without this hard work, a dream will remain only a desire in the subconscious mind and will never be achieved.

Believe

*"Believe in yourself and then live so as
to reach your possibilities."*

—Thomas S. Monson[1]

The next step in creating your plan is to start believing that you can reach your dreams. Now that you have recorded what you want, you must start believing you can achieve it. Anytime you start dreaming, doubt enters your mind. You may think of the obstacles, challenges, and trials that await you or that will slow you from reaching your dream. This is when you cast all doubt aside and start believing that anything is possible.

Now is the moment to clean out all that is negative in your mind and speech and pour in only positive. This is the moment you train your brain to think, "Yes, I can" and "Yes, I will."

The best musicians, athletes, or experts in any profession are successful at what they do because of repetition. Repetition is the key to training your mind, muscles, and even your soul. The more you do something, the easier it is.

Start today. Think only positive thoughts. Make sure anything you say is only positive, and practice this every day for a month. You will be surprised at the difference it will make in your life and the lives of those around you.

Your thoughts are powerful, and even when you start to believe, you may begin to doubt yourself at times. The power of your thoughts can help or hinder your plan. So stop any negative thoughts, eliminate any negative feelings, and keep telling yourself, "Yes, I can."

Surround Yourself with Greatness

Surround yourself with people you want to be like. If you surround yourself with negative people who criticize and speak negatively, then you will find yourself acting like them. If you surround yourself with positive, inspirational people, then you will be like them. Who do you spend most of your time with?

Write down five people you spend most of your time with.

1. _____

2. _____

3. _____

4. _____

5. _____

Are these five people helping you achieve greatness? Do they bring out the best in you? Do they have the same values you have, and do they support you? Are they the type of people that have attributes and qualities you seek? If not, then you may need to adjust the time spent with them and find those who will help you reach your ultimate goals and dreams.

Make Good Choices

Elder Dallin H. Oaks said, "As we consider various choices, we should remember that it is not enough that something is good. Other choices are better, and still others are best. Even though a particular choice is more costly, its far greater value may make it the best choice of all. Consider how we use our time in the choices we make in viewing television, playing video games, surfing the Internet, or reading books or magazines. Of course it is good to view wholesome entertainment or to obtain interesting information. But not everything of that sort is worth the portion of our life we give to obtain it. Some things are better, and others are best."[2]

Everyone has been blessed with abilities and talents. We are all in this world making choices about how to use these skills. It is important to identify what talents you have. What things do you do very well?

1. _____
2. _____
3. _____

What are the three best choices you've made in your life?

1. _____
2. _____
3. _____

What are the worst choices you have made in your life? (If you don't want to write them down here, then think privately of what they are.)

_____

_____

_____

Why did you make these bad choices? (Circle one of these possible reasons.)

1. I failed to stand up for what I believe in.
2. I wanted to follow my friends, be accepted, and just went along.
3. I made this choice in private and hid it from others because I knew it was wrong.
4. I was lazy.
5. I cared what other people thought of me.
6. I was angry, frustrated, and mad.
7. I was not fully committed to something. I had one foot in and one foot out of the deal.
8. I just quit.

9. I wanted to hurt somebody, pay them back, or get even.
10. I did it basically because people (parents, friends, leaders, teachers) told me not to do it. I rebelled.

Human potential is unlimited, and everyone is capable of great things.

Great things come from both small ideas and big dreams. The key is to trust yourself and trust your abilities and capabilities. Many of us have big dreams, yet so many times, distractions stop us from pursuing them.

Your life is a road map, and you are the driver of your dreams. When you have a direction, and you are passionate about your dreams, you will create ways and means to reach them. In order to be effective and use all your potential in the right manner, you must draw a map to your destination—you need a strategy to reach your target.

Imagine trying to go to the grocery store without knowing how to get there. You may lose your way many times, get frustrated or stressed out, and inflict your frustration on others. You may never reach your destination, or you will reach it only after much wasted time.

When you plan and have a map, you move smoothly and happily and reach your destination in a healthy and timely manner. Along the way, you might encounter a traffic jam or other delays that are outside your control, but if you accept these challenges as fun and adventurous, you can stay motivated until you reach your destination.

Believe in yourself and believe you can cross mountains, ford rivers, and conquer obstacles with civility. Learn from people who have succeeded and, most important, remember to use every experience to better yourself and grow. You can do it. You are a son or daughter of our Heavenly Father. You are royalty.

Set Goals

Write Down Your Goals

Agoal not written down is only a wish.

How do you set goals and reach them? You have to write goals down. If you don't, they are easily lost, as is your sense of direction. A special thing happens when you write down your goals: your mind, body, spirit, and all you have and do is pointed in one direction. You think, ponder, and begin to move toward that goal without even knowing it. Write down your goals and see the magic that comes with the act. Make sure your goals are specific, motivational, achievable, relevant to you, and have a time frame attached.

In Luke 2:52, we learn that from the time Jesus was twelve years old until he turned thirty, he increased in *wisdom* and *stature,* before *God* and *man.* This basically describes the four primary areas where your mind and your goals should be focused.

Wisdom: receive education and stay educated.

Stature: stay physically strong and healthy.

Man: use social skills to improve your interpersonal relationships.

God: set spiritual goals to help you grow closer to the Savior and God the Father.

Make a list of five goals you want to achieve and focus on. Take into account your dreams and values. These five goals need to be very important to you; you must be committed to achieving them.

Now create a game plan for how you will achieve each goal. Be specific. The more detailed you can make this game plan, the clearer it will become to you. You will know exactly what changes you need to make in your habits, thoughts, actions, and life to get where you want to be.

 Scan this QR code (or visit http://youtu.be/WpBKwc 6DtYO) for tips from Travis on how to set goals.

GOAL 1

Name three actions this goal requires of you. For example, if I wanted to play basketball at a high level, I would need to practice every day. This is when you start to get specific and break down the "how I will reach my goals" into steps. If basketball practice is my goal, I need to specifically write down how many hours it will take each day, what drills I will do, and how many repetitions I will do in the time allotted for this goal. I need to evaluate my skills compared to others and determine what I need to focus on. If my shooting is good but my ball handling is bad, then I need to spend more time on dribbling the ball.

Again, be specific and very detailed in what you must do to make this goal come true. Repeat this step for all five goals.

ACTION 1

1. _____
2. _____
3. _____

ACTION 2

1. _____
2. _____
3. _____

ACTION 3

1. _____
2. _____
3. _____

GOAL 2

_____

ACTION 1

1. _____

2. _____
3. _____

ACTION 2

1. _____
2. _____
3. _____

ACTION 3

1. _____
2. _____
3. _____

GOAL 3

_____

ACTION 1

1. _____
2. _____
3. _____

ACTION 2

1. _____
2. _____
3. _____

ACTION 3

1. _____
2. _____
3. _____

GOAL 4

_____

ACTION 1

1. _____
2. _____
3. _____

ACTION 2

1. _____
2. _____
3. _____

ACTION 3

1. _____
2. _____
3. _____

GOAL 5

_____

ACTION 1

1. _____
2. _____
3. _____

ACTION 2

1. _____
2. _____
3. _____

ACTION 3

1. _____

2. _____

3. _____

Here is a list of five easy ways to help you achieve your goals:

1. **Simplify:** Choose a small, specific goal, or break up larger goals into small pieces that can be done on a daily basis. Big successes start with little ones.

2. **Write it down:** Write your goal in large letters and place it where you will see it several times a day. Putting your goal to paper makes it official: You want it!

3. **Keep track every day:** This step is very important. If you don't keep track of your daily progress, you won't progress. Everything we accomplish requires daily steps which turn the goal into a habit.

4. **Really want it:** If you don't really want to do it, you won't succeed. Pick goals you want to achieve, or change your attitude so you really do want it.

5. **Schedule time:** Here are three ideas to help you make time for your goal:

    Prioritize: Make time by not doing things that are of less, or no, value. Hours spent in front of the TV or computer can be used more productively by just pushing the off button or walking away. Sometimes you may even need to limit the nonproductive time you spend with your friends, whether on the phone, texting, or at school.

Say no: Learn to gracefully say no to those who ask for your time when you already have too much to do. Saying no can be done in a kind way; just be clear that you cannot do what is being asked of you.

Make the time: You have to *make* the time or you won't *make* the goal. Pick a time when you will work on your goal, such as early in the morning, late at night, or during lunch. If you "just don't have the time," then wake up earlier.

Overcoming Your Fears

One of the biggest hurdles in the way of reaching your goals will be fear. You fear failure, you fear what people think, you fear having to make a commitment and write it down and be accountable for doing it or not doing it. Other hurdles include procrastination, laziness, and doubt.

These hurdles can be faced, recognized, and overcome by sticking with your plan. Remember, you are amazing, you are capable, and you can carve a path to reach your dreams.

Everybody is afraid of something. Missionaries sometimes fear they don't know enough about the gospel to do a good job, or they fear what strangers might think of them.

Many athletes fear failure—that they won't compete or match up against other talented teammates or opponents.

What is your biggest fear? Are you afraid of change or making a commitment? Are you afraid of disappointing somebody? Is it your parents? Your friends? Your brothers or sisters, leaders, teachers? Face these fears, get them out in the open and see them for what they are. They are your enemy, they are holding you back, and they need to be addressed and attacked.

Write them down here:

_____

_____

_____

_____

_____

Now that you have identified your fears, take them on. If you have a fear of talking to new people, then go talk to someone new every day until your fear goes away. If you stop doing it for a while, that fear may come back and you will need to attack it again. When we go after our fears, we need to identify things we can do that help us overcome those fears. You cannot overcome a fear unless you know and understand that fear. Look at this as finding the proper weapons and strategies to battle that particular fear.

Make a list of possible ways to overcome your fears:

_____

_____

_____

_____

_____

Celebrate Your Victories

It's time to celebrate! Celebrate milestones, successes, and your courage to get out of your comfort zone. Celebrate overcoming even the smallest fears. Celebrate the growth you are gaining and know that you are on the path of making your dreams come true.

Write down two milestones or successes you have accomplished recently:

1. _____
2. _____

Who Is Driving You?

Now, answer this question about some of your choices: If your choice were compared to a car, would you have been the driver or a passenger?

A driver is in charge. He or she takes the wheel and controls the speed, direction, and even the radio.

A passenger is along for the ride and lets the driver take them wherever the driver wants to go.

You know "drivers" in your life. You may even be one.

These are people who are in control; they know what they want to do and where they are going. They lead out and stand for ideals and principles that have weight. Other people look up to them.

List five people you really admire. Then list a character trait you admire in them.

Name	Character Trait
1. _____	_____
2. _____	_____
3. _____	_____
4. _____	_____
5. _____	_____

The people above have made an impression on you. There are reasons why. You can make similar impressions on others as you take charge of your life, make good choices, and eliminate bad choices.

Don't Blame Others

"When you blame others,
you give up your power to change."

—Dr. Robert Anthony[3]

We can all get past the point of blaming others. We can gain knowledge, experience, and self-confidence, and obtain the true joy, peace, and happiness that we seek.

When we are faced with trials—and we all are—we have two choices: Either become better or let them destroy us. Blaming others is a waste of time. No matter how much fault you find in others, it will not change you. If you take your life into your own hands, what happens? Something special: there is no one to blame! Where does the power lie? In you!

Hero Within

Plan of Action

"All these primary impulses, not easily described in words, are the springs of man's actions."

—Albert Einstein[4]

The most important key to achieving your goals is action. You may have more talents and gifts than anyone in the world, but without action you are destined to never reach your goals and your true potential.

At a basic level, each of us knows how important action is. Write down what you did today.

Morning

_____

_____

Afternoon

_____

_____

Evening

_____

_____

Out of all the activities you did today, which ones are distracting you from accomplishing your goals? Commit yourself to a "stop doing" list right now.

STOP DOING

_____

_____

_____

Everyone needs a plan of action. You can create one. There are little things you can do daily that will change your life in the long run. Over time these daily actions will shape who you are in a positive way.

Here is a list of possible actions that can help make you a driver instead of a passenger. You can add to this list. Pick and choose which ones you can begin doing today. I promise you, doing a handful of these things will change your life faster than you realize. Taking action makes a difference; it pushes you forward moment by moment.

A Simple Action Plan

- Make a to-do list and check off items when you take care of them.
- Read a book about somebody famous you admire.
- Reduce or even stop the minutes/hours you spend playing video games.
- Run from and avoid pornography in all its forms (TV, movies, magazines, Internet).
- Go to church ten to fifteen minutes early and listen to the prelude music.
- Be the first to volunteer. Make it a race to be first in line.
- Dogs need to expend energy. Find someone who has a dog and walk that dog.
- Tell a friend or parent how you feel about some topic. Listen to what they say.
- If you are a guy, get a haircut, shave, and save enough money to buy a suit. Wear it to church and be proud of the fact you want to look like your local bishop, other Church leaders, and the prophet.
- Find music that lifts you up and turn it on while you work.
- Randomly pick one thing you can do to help around the house and do it without being asked.

- Pick one of the unhealthiest things you eat and stop eating it.
- Start a journal, write in it daily, even just a sentence or two. Add pictures and drawings to your journal.
- Choose a person who is away from you and write them a letter or card.
- Take a walk for ten or fifteen minutes every day. Breathe deeply several times and enjoy your surroundings.
- Learn to cook something new.
- Create a project to do—big or small. Start and finish it.
- Identify three things that absolutely make you feel the Spirit. Write them down.
- Pick out someone with few friends and strike up a conversation.
- Go up to a leader or teacher and tell them thanks for what they do.
- Memorize, word for word, a scripture. Set a goal to memorize a scripture a week.
- Begin a collection of your favorite quotes or stories and put them in a folder.
- Record on a calendar each time you say a prayer.
- Write down three projects you want to do. Start one, and when it's finished, start another.
- Find time to read every day.
- Give someone a compliment every day.

- Get up an hour earlier than normal for a week. Use that hour in a good way.
- Teach something you have a passion for to another person.
- Take up a new hobby or sport.
- Be humble. If someone gives you a compliment, say "thank you" and look them in the eye.
- Play with your little brother or sister, niece or nephew, or find a little child and spend ten minutes on the ground with them.
- When you walk into a room, smile and be happy.
- Learn to play a musical instrument.
- Bear your testimony this month and invite someone to do it with you.
- Take time to learn about a new career and interview a person who has that career.

Values Matter

While you are determining your dreams, goals, fears, what you want, and how you will get there, you must also determine *why* you want it. This is an important and crucial step to achieving true peace and happiness. If your dreams and your goals do not align with your values, then you are destined to eventually fail.

Look back at your dreams and goals. Look at what you want and why you want it. If it doesn't align with your values, then you will want to make adjustments to better align your dreams with your values.

Defining our values gives us purpose and direction. When you don't know or you haven't clearly defined your values, you end up drifting along in life. Instead of basing your decisions on an internal compass, you make choices based on circumstances and social pressures. You end up trying to fulfill other people's expectations instead of your own. Before you know it, life has passed you by, and you haven't even started to live. Living without core values is exhausting and leaves you feeling empty and lost. Conversely, living a life in line with your core values brings purpose, direction, joy, true peace, and happiness.

Defining our values enables us to make fewer bad choices. Perhaps you have a vague idea about what you value. But if you haven't clearly defined your values, you can end up making choices that conflict with them. When your actions conflict with your values, the result is unhappiness and frustration.

Defining our values gives us confidence. I've noticed that when I take the time to really think and meditate upon what I value as a man and write those things down, I'm more likely to have the courage and confidence to make choices based on those values. There's something about actually writing down your values that makes you more committed to living them.

Hard Work

Success is the reward of hard work. A lazy man seldom succeeds. This is a universal truth. There is another saying: "Fortune favors the brave." In this world of ours, one cannot be successful if one is not prepared to work hard.

L.A. Dodgers coach Tommy Lasorda often repeated the Latin proverb, "The difference between the impossible and the possible lies in a person's determination."

Take the example of many young athletes. They did not earn their fame overnight. To achieve this they had to work day and night for years, sometimes forgetting their pleasures and happiness.

We cannot passively try to fix a problem or complete a job. At some point we need to look it straight in the eye and get it done.

All the so-called "Secrets to Success" work only if you are willing to.

Yes, you have to dream big, set goals, make choices, believe in yourself, and never ever give up. But all of these tools are useless without hard work.

Be a Leader

"Leaders are not born; they are made."

—Vince Lombardi[5]

Great leaders solve problems, see the big picture, are positive, make decisions, take responsibility, have vision, are the best teachers, and know that life is not all about them.

Take Inventory—
I Want to Be Like . . .

Everyone needs an example in their life—everyone needs a leader. Particularly in this life, people need to look toward a leader—they need to look to you. Think about the great leaders you have met throughout your life and make a list of the qualities and attributes you admire most about them.

Look for opportunities to lead. Whether it is in Scouting, sports, church, school, or at home, you can be a great example to many friends and acquaintances who watch you and often times will follow your footsteps. Your courage and desire to lead will come as you live the standards of the Church, stay close to the Spirit, strive to make good decisions, and follow the Savior Jesus Christ.

List five things you can do to be a leader.

1. _____
2. _____
3. _____
4. _____
5. _____

List five reasons you want to be a leader.

1. _____
2. _____
3. _____
4. _____
5. _____

List five great leaders you know.

1. _____

2. _____

3. _____

4. _____

5. _____

To be a great leader, you must develop those attributes that are esteemed and looked highly upon. Some of these may include honesty; integrity; loyalty; having a positive attitude; being solution-focused versus obstacle-focused; being a good communicator, a hard worker, and someone who is compassionate and truly cares about others. These are characteristics that most people want to emulate and look for in their leaders. You need to be this type of person. You are not being asked to change who you are, but rather, to improve and grow.

Teach Others

*"Let us think of education as the means of
developing our greatest abilities, because in each of us
there is a private hope and dream which, fulfilled, can
be translated into benefit for everyone and
greater strength for our Nation."*

—John F. Kennedy[6]

Your role as a leader is more important than you can imagine. Now that you have created a plan, set goals, and found the hero within, you can teach others to do the same.

You limit yourself when you don't teach others; but when you do, you enable yourself to give what you have learned and experienced. Every day you can wake up and think, Who am I going to help today? Who am I going to teach today?

Write down five people you will teach how to create a plan, set goals, and find the hero within.

1. _____

2. _____

3. _____

4. _____

5. _____

Remember, great leadership has nothing to do with a title or reward; rather, it is your ability to influence others in a positive way. Make sure you complete the exercises and review the principles taught in this workbook. As you do, they will become habits, help you reach your true potential, and ultimately change your life and the lives of those around you.

Acknowledgments

I am deeply grateful to many who have helped me make this book possible. My sentiment is aptly expressed by the novelist George Moore, who said, "A man travels the world over in search of what he needs and returns home to find it."[1] So it is with this book. It could not have been written without the help of many people for whom I am deeply thankful and express my love.

Special thanks to the talented Dick Harmon for his magnificent assistance in every part of this endeavor, particularly his insights to writing. Without his creative help, we'd still be talking about this book instead of reading it.

Special thanks to:

LaRee Hansen, for her love, charity, kindness, counsel, friendship, remarkable ideas, boldness, and willingness to support me through every facet of life. You are my best friend and I love you.

Ryder, Mason, and Halle, for their kindness, love, and unwavering support. And for running to the door when I return home from a long day and saying, "Daddy, I love you." I love you more.

With deep gratitude, I acknowledge my parents, Scott and the late Laurie Hansen, for their love and profound influence on my life, and my stepmother, Lori. I acknowledge my brothers, Tyler and Landon, and my baby sisters, Heather and Hollie, for their friendship, love, and relationships with my wife and children, and my stepsisters, Karly and Sarah. I acknowledge my other parents, David and Ruth Merrell, for treating me like a son and for their amazing examples of charity and kindness. I also acknowledge many, many other family members, leaders, and friends, for their influence on my life, my thinking, and the development of this book.

Most important, I acknowledge and thank my Heavenly Father and Savior Jesus Christ for the blessings, insights, and support I have felt throughout this project and my life.

Notes

INTRODUCTION

1. James Freeman Clarke, in *Elbert Hubbard's Scrap Book* [1923], 95.
2. Gordon B. Hinckley, "Stay on the High Road," *Ensign,* May 2004, 112–13.

CHAPTER 3

1. Jimmer Fredette, in Pat Forde, *The Contract* (Salt Lake City: Shadow Mountain, 2012), 6.

CHAPTER 4

1. Gordon B. Hinckley, "The War We Are Winning," *Ensign,* November 1986, 42, 44.

CHAPTER 6

1. Abraham Lincoln, in Caroline Hanks Hitchcock, *Nancy Hanks: The Story of Abraham Lincoln's Mother* (New York: Doubleday & McClure Co., 1899), 105.
2. Abraham Lincoln, quoted in Marvin J. Ashton, "'The Word Is Commitment,'" *Ensign,* November, 1983, 61.

CHAPTER 7

1. Gordon B. Hinckley, in "Pres. Hinckley in Chile marks largest LDS gathering," *Church News,* May 8, 1999.
2. Ibid.
3. See "God Be with You Till We Meet Again," in *Hymns of The Church of Jesus*

Christ of Latter-day Saints (Salt Lake City: The Church of Jesus Christ of Latter-day Saints, 1985), no. 152.

CHAPTER 12

1. Ezra Taft Benson, "Born of God," *Ensign,* July 1989, 4.

CHAPTER 13

1. "BYU Stages Incredible Comeback in Provo," BYU Men's Basketball Game Notes, Game #18 vs. the University of Utah, January 25, 2003, 3.
2. Gordon B. Hinckley, "'Great Shall Be the Peace of Thy Children,'" *Ensign,* November 2000, 52.

CHAPTER 14

1. See http://www.americanadoptions.com/adoption/celebrity_adoption.

CHAPTER 15

1. Gordon B. Hinckley, "An Ensign to the Nations, A Light to the World," *Ensign,* November 2003, 83, 85.
2. *Merriam-Webster's Collegiate Dictionary,* tenth edition, s.v. "hero."

WORKBOOK

1. Thomas S. Monson, "Living the Abundant Life," *Liahona,* January 2012, 5.
2. Dallin H. Oaks, "Good, Better, Best," *Ensign,* November 2007, 104–5.
3. Robert Anthony, *Think Big: A Think Collection* (New York: Berkley, 1999), 22.
4. Albert Einstein, *Out of My Later Years* (Estate of Albert Einstein, 1956), 15.
5. Vince Lombardi, in Vince Lombardi Jr., *What It Takes to Be #1: Vince Lombardi on Leadership* (New York: McGraw-Hill, 2001), 37.
6. John F. Kennedy: "Proclamation 3422–American Education Week, 1961," Online by Gerhard Peters and John T. Woolley, *The American Presidency Project.* http://www.presidency.ucsb.edu/ws/?pid=24146.

ACKNOWLEDGMENTS

1. George Moore, *The Brook Kerith* (New York: Macmillan Company, 1916), 122.

About the Author

TRAVIS HANSEN grew up in Orem, Utah, and served an LDS mission in Santiago, Chile. He returned to play basketball at BYU and was named the conference defensive player of the year as a senior. He was drafted by the Atlanta Hawks to play in the NBA, and he also played professionally in Spain and Russia. Travis and his wife, LaRee, started the Little Heroes Foundation to improve the lives of children around the world.